DIY vegan

Nicole Axworthy
and Lisa Pitman

DIY vegan

More Than 100 Easy Recipes to Create an Awesome Plant-Based Pantry

St. Martin's Griffin
New York

www.stmartins.com

Photography by Nicole Axworthy

Food Styling by Nicole Axworthy and Lisa Pitman

Author photo by Amber Ellis

Designed by Steven Seighman

The Library of Congress Cataloging-in-Publication Data is available upon request.

ISBN 978-1-250-05871-3 (trade paperback)
ISBN 978-1-4668-8690-2 (e-book)

St. Martin's Griffin books may be purchased for educational, business, or promotional use. For information on bulk purchases, please contact the Macmillan Corporate and Premium Sales Department at 1-800-221-7945, extension 5442, or write to specialmarkets@macmillan.com.

First Edition: October 2015

10 9 8 7 6 5 4 3 2 1

Contents

· · · · · · · · · · · ·

Note to Readers

· ·

THERE IS GELATIN in Frosted Mini-Wheats?!

Yes, there is, and milk protein in nondairy coffee creamer.

Seem ridiculous? We think so.

Welcome to *DIY Vegan*. We wrote this book to save you from wasting untold time reading labels and dreaming of the day when a new vegan mayo finds its way to the shelves of your small-town grocery store. Because we've been there, too. Between the two of us, we've racked up more than forty years of eating a vegan diet. We love almost everything about being vegan, with one exception: scouring the ingredient list of every package for hidden dairy and other non-vegan ingredients.

But reading labels is just something we had to do. Lisa, an energetic idealist, was all of six years old when she went vegan—at first for health reasons because her body couldn't digest animal protein—and decades later, her commitment to compassion remains steadfast. Nicole, a driven, empathetic activist, went vegetarian in her early teens after learning about the fate of animals in the food industry and then adopted veganism soon after. At the time we started on this path, it was rare to see the word *vegan* on the cover of a cookbook, let alone on a label in a supermarket.

We were both young and enthusiastic. We committed to veganism before we even knew how to cook. So, at first we relied on pasta with tomato sauce, peanut butter sandwiches, and plenty of fruit and vegetables. Whenever we wanted to try something new, it meant checking the ingredient lists with our fingers crossed. Sometimes we lucked out; sometimes words like *caseinate, lactose,* or *whey* showed up and ruined all the fun. We both knew that for veganism to be a healthful, joyful lifestyle for the rest of our days, we needed to find a way to do it without feeling deprived. We needed to enjoy the foods we love—by finding options created with compassion that would also do our bodies some good. Seems simple, right?

The best thing about becoming vegan before it was cool was being a pioneer in creating a whole new plant-based cuisine. As the saying goes, necessity is the mother of invention. Well, when you're the only vegan you've ever known, the opportunities for invention abound. So we learned to play in the kitchen. When our friends were eating meat and potatoes, we were trying out dhals, *mesir wats*, black bean enchiladas, falafel sandwiches, *bibimbap*, and all the kinds of kale.

We quickly discovered that vegan food meant an abundance of diverse, delicious flavors and limitless possibilities, but the convenience food industry clearly didn't see it that way. Who knew the intriguing Pop-Tart's flavor that looked so good on TV contained fat from the abdomen of pigs (lard), cows' connective tissue (gelatin), ground-up insects (carmine), high-fructose corn syrup, the illusive TBHQ, and "natural flavor"?

Sound appetizing? Not to us, and probably not to you, either.

Once our comfort with vegan cooking grew, so did our culinary goals. Ironically, this was also around the time veganism started growing in popularity, and we began to see more and more processed vegan products hitting the shelves. As excited as we were for their arrival and availability, reviewing their ingredient lists demonstrated that vegan doesn't always mean healthy. Not to say that we haven't reveled in the enjoyment of a vegan peanut butter cup or a pint of coconut ice cream, but those foods are treats for us, not staples.

We decided we didn't want to be tied to the products that might be available in our grocery store (depending on the store manager's whims . . . fingers crossed that he has a vegan cousin) or delivered through airmail. We wanted to be able to eat fantastic, healthful food wherever and whenever we wanted.

Are we just a little demanding? Maybe. Determined? Absolutely.

Our challenge: to create nourishing recipes that fit into our busy schedules and could be reproduced in almost any kitchen around the world.

And so began our experiments to create yummy snacks, treats, meals, and sides, many of which we've shared on our blogs, VeganCulinaryCrusade.com and ADashofCompassion.com, and through our e-cookbooks, *Tiny Treats* and *Edible Gifts*. We learned to make our own nondairy milk, created flour out of almond pulp and oat groats, piped tiny chocolate chips from homemade cacao, and cheered on our food processor while it ground peanuts into a smooth, silky butter.

After years of testing and perfecting, we're ready to share our secrets with you. This book is full of our discoveries—the ways we reimagined recipes with real ingredients that amp up the flavor and nutrition. In the following chapters, we have 135 new recipes for everyday staples that you can make in your own kitchens from ingredients available down the street (whether that be in Paris, Toronto, or Melbourne), everything from DIY milks, flours, and butters to fun and easy-to-adapt sauces, spreads, and snack foods.

Ultimately, we want to redefine today's vegan kitchen, lining shelves with glass mason jars and reusable containers instead of cardboard cereal boxes and plastic cartons, and we want you to feel comfortable and confident that you can fill your pantry with food you can trust.

WHY DIY?

Because we can. And you can, too!

The first question people ask when they find out you're vegan is: "What do you eat?" It's hard for most to imagine a diet without eggs, dairy, and meat when every label you read on grocery store shelves seems to contain ingredients like whey, milk powder, or butterfat (and that's just in the cracker aisle). Vegans often become experts in analyzing labels: for every new product you come across, the first thing you'll do is scan the ingredient list to confirm whether it contains animal-derived ingredients—never mind the other impossible-to-pronounce preservatives, stabilizers, artificial colors, and chemical sweeteners.

But we've got a solution: do it yourself. You can make it better, healthier, and often cheaper than anything you can buy. And no labels to read.

We also DIY because:

- **We save money.** It might seem that convenience foods are cheaper, and if you're not concerned about quality, that can sometimes be the case. But most of the time, we pay more for ready-to-eat items. On almond milk and almond butter alone, we've saved enough over the years to pay for special evenings out at our favorite restaurants, where we're happy for someone else to do the cooking and the dishes. We buy many of our staple ingredients in bulk, getting just what we need without all the packaging and brand names. We rely on versatile ingredients that can be used in a multitude of recipes, ensuring that we make the most of them while they're still fresh.

- **We save time.** This may seem like an impossible statement in a book about making things from scratch, but truly, we spend less time shopping and cooking than before. The recipes in this book have become our roadmap—they are tried and tested to provide reliable results. We stock up on staple ingredients and make everything we need on a regular cycle; we don't spend a lot of time thinking about our shopping list or standing with the cupboards open trying to pick a snack now that we have a plan.

- **We feel better.** We've stopped unknowingly consuming sugar, salt, and preservatives. It wasn't a conscious avoidance effort. It just happened along the way, and the result is more energy, stronger immunity, and bodies that wake up ready for another adventure every day. We didn't say we don't consume sugar or salt, just not the stuff hidden in a long ingredient list. We happily add maple syrup to our pancakes and salt to our simmering sauces. We do it for flavor and add just what we need to bring out the best of the ingredients.

- **We can do it anywhere.** We both love to travel. But being away from home also means being away from familiar foods. Knowing how to make your favorite snacks and meals from scratch means you can leave behind the anxiety about finding vegan-friendly foods when you head off to visit Ecuador, Indonesia, or even your in-laws.

- **We enjoy our food more.** We're proud of the food we make and we know everything it contains has something good to offer. We eat more consciously, with more appreciation and, since we've figured out 135 recipes we love, with more enjoyment. Truly, homemade tomato sauce shames the stuff from the store, fresh almond milk doesn't have any strange aftertaste, and fresh-baked granola has a crunch and complexity that far surpasses any store-bought cereal.

- **We get to share.** The best thing about making homemade staples is that they are already perfect for sharing as an incredibly thoughtful gift. Trust us, showing up at a party with a batch of vanilla ice cream, caramelized chai popcorn, salsa verde, or pico de gallo that you made yourself garners a whole lot more gratitude than a bag of Oreo cookies you picked up on your way. Plus, we believe people bond over food, and that one of the greatest gifts you can share is a nourishing meal with a friend or loved one. So we strongly encourage you to share the secrets you've discovered in these pages and the beautiful food you've crafted yourself.

WHY VEGAN AND GLUTEN-FREE?

Plant-based diets are the fastest-growing dietary trend, and smart people like you are seeking alternatives to processed products. With increasing awareness of celiac disease and more mainstream interest in avoiding wheat, we've made sure each made-at-home solution has an option for everyone.

EASY-TO-FIND INGREDIENTS

We're also hoping to earn the "exceeds expectations" gold star for creating every recipe in this book with easy-to-find, whole-food ingredients. To make these recipes, we didn't order

Our family and friends are used to being presented with bags of carefully curated freezer-friendly food. If you invite either of us over, you should expect we will have made something special for the occasion.

I think I say "I love you" with muffins. When someone I know is pregnant, while they're nesting and readying themselves for the new arrival, I'm filling my freezer with black bean burritos, savory soups, veggie burgers, muffins, and cookies—all the things you can eat single-handed. There is nothing like delivering a stack of homemade snacks to a woman who's about to become a mom. It is the most amazing thing to be able to make the life of a new mother a little bit easier—with ready-to-eat, healthful, delicious food. —L. P.

At work, I think every big decision should be accompanied by a baked good, something sweet to savor while you weigh all the options. I often arrive with a basket of snacks because I'd rather be known for that than my proofreading skills. My husband's colleagues have started sending requests. It makes me smile to think that, rather than call in a caterer or stop at the store, they prefer to order homemade favorites from me. —N. A.

any special ingredients online. We went to the grocery stores and health food stores in our neighborhoods and used what we could find—with a lot of creativity and some almost delusional determination. Of course, ingredient availability will differ depending on where you live. If you can't find what you need in your usual grocery store, try the health food store, bulk food store, or Asian/Southeast Asian markets, or, as a last resort, stock up online or the next time you travel to a big city.

HOW CAN YOU MAKE DIY WORK WITH YOUR 9 TO 5?

As much as we would love to fill our days with checking in on our soaking nuts, piping swirls of chocolate frosting, and playing with pulsing different versions of pesto, we both have busy lives that mostly keep us away from home. We spend more time typing than stirring. But that doesn't mean we have to settle for shelf-stable convenience meals. Life is just too short to eat something that could outlive you. We want fresh, flavorful food. So, how do we fit it all in? The best surprise about working on a make-it-all-from-scratch cookbook while keeping up with our full-time jobs, families, love lives, etc., was the realization that the secret to having it all is *habit*.

Most of the recipes in this book actually take very little hands-on time. With a little planning and a different shopping list, you can fill your pantry without filling up all your free time.

There are many recipes in this book you can easily make on a whim. If you decide it's pizza night at four P.M., no problem. You can have the pizza dough and pizza sauce ready to serve by six.

But if you want to replace your regular store-bought ingredients with self-crafted staples, we suggest setting up a regular routine. You can set aside a little time every weekend to whip up these foods and then enjoy the results over the next couple of weeks.

Your go-to recipes may be different from ours, but here are some basic examples of how you might set up your pantry cycle.

Weekly:
- Blend fresh almond milk (page 38)
- Culture coconut yogurt (page 45)
- Bake a loaf of bread (page 79)

Biweekly:
- Shake up some salad dressing (pages 113–116)
- Bake a batch of granola or mix up some muesli (pages 68–71, 75)
- Process some almond butter or chocolate hazelnut spread (pages 106, 109)
- Pulse some mac and cheese sauce, popcorn spice blends, and parmesan shakers (pages 159, 166–168)

Monthly:
- Craft some artisanal cheeses (pages 49–58)
- Make your must-have condiments, like ketchup, mayo, or mustard (pages 141, 145–146)
- Stir up some snack bars (pages 89–90)
- Simmer some tomato sauce, peanut sauce, or nacho sauce (pages 130, 135–136)
- Freeze homemade ice cream or frozen yogurt (pages 62–65)

Every Six Months:
- Create fresh spice blends (pages 170–174)
- Start a new batch of vanilla extract (page 192)
- Mix up your gluten-free flour mix (page 179)
- Fill some jars with ready-to-use muffin mix and cake mix (pages 180, 183)

The real strategy for successfully switching to more DIY staples is taking the extra few minutes to soak some cashews before you leave for work or to stir up your overnight oats before you head to bed. A little attention in advance makes amazing food possible later.

Now with your DIY instruction manual in hand, it's time to pick a project and stock up on supplies. We'll meet you by the mason jars.

Love & cupcakes,
Lisa & Nicole

DIY vegan

CHAPTER 1

Stocking Your Awesome Vegan Pantry

· ·

THE FIRST STEP TO CRAFTING your staples at home is filling your shelves with all the essential ingredients for a productive vegan pantry. Here, we're going to introduce you to a roster of versatile superstars: whole grains, nuts, seeds, oils, dried fruit, sweeteners, and spices.

While this is not a complete list of food you might want in your kitchen or pantry, it includes essential ingredients featured in the recipes in this book. Once you have these on hand, you are ready to re-create all your everyday favorites, like the creamer you use in your morning coffee or the crackers you pack for snacks, and to make your vegan kitchen complete!

You don't need to rush out and get everything on this list today. Start with a recipe or two, and you'll begin to recognize the more common ingredients and see their potential. Soon they'll go from weird, health-food hippie ingredients to items you can't live without.

WHOLE GRAINS, FLOURS & STARCHES

We're not telling you to throw out your old basics like white rice and all-purpose flour when stocking your pantry, but there are all sorts of grains and flours that will each bring a little something extra to your cooking, including plant-powered nutrients and delicious, wholesome flavors.

Almond meal & flour: Almond meal and almond flour lend a soft, chewy texture and nutty flavor to baked goods. Almond meal is made from raw almonds with the skins intact and has a slightly coarse texture, while almond flour is made from blanched almonds (which have been heated to remove their skins) and has a delicate and fine texture. Almond flour can also be made by dehydrating the almond pulp leftover from making nut milk. In most cases, we use almond meal but both can be made in your own kitchen (see page 190).

Arrowroot: Yes, it's made from a root called arrowroot (no creativity here at all). Use it where you'd use cornstarch—it thickens sauces and puddings and helps bind and crisp up the texture of baked goods.

Brown rice flour: This popular gluten-free flour is made from finely milled brown rice and is part of our Gluten-Free Flour Mix (page 179). Look for brown rice flour at bulk and health food stores and in the specialty food section of large grocers.

Brown rice (puffed): A light and crunchy way to enjoy the goodness of brown rice, this puffed version is used in the Snackworthy Cereal Bars on page 90 and the Cinnamon Toast Cereal on page 73. We love Nature's Path and Arrowhead Mills brands, which contain only one ingredient (puffed brown rice!) and can be found at most health food stores and large grocers.

Buckwheat groats & flour: Even though it has "wheat" right in the name, buckwheat is not even related to regular wheat. In fact, it's gluten-free. (Who the heck is in charge of naming these things, anyway?) Raw buckwheat groats are the hulled seeds of the buckwheat plant, as opposed to kasha, which is toasted and much darker in color. Raw groats provide a wonderful crunchy texture to recipes when used whole, or a soft, pleasant flavor when made into flour. You can find the groats and flour at bulk and health food stores.

Chickpea flour: Otherwise known as garbanzo bean flour, this pale yellow flour is made from ground chickpeas. It imparts a sweet, almost beany flavor and aroma, which isn't quite as pronounced after baking. Because it's made from one of our favorite legumes and is high in protein, we've incorporated it in the Gluten-Free Flour Mix on page 179. Look for chickpea flour at bulk and health food stores.

Cornmeal: This common staple is made from dried corn. We prefer organic, stone-ground cornmeal and use it in some recipes to add a little crunch, like the Creamy Five-Grain Porridge on page 74, or for the bottom of homemade pizza crust (pages 154 and 157).

Millet & millet flour: While most gluten-free grains have a strong underlying flavor, millet is an exception to the rule. We sometimes grind whole millet to add a crunchy texture to recipes like the Pancake Mix on page 151, but millet flour is excellent for lighter baked goods that require a texture and flavor similar to wheat (which is why our Ultimate Gluten-Free Bread on page 79 tastes so good). You can find both the whole grain and flour at bulk and health food stores.

Oats (rolled) & oat flour: Oats are one of our favorite grains. They're wholesome, fiber-rich, and have far more uses than just oatmeal (think quick breads, cookies, and pancakes). Oat flour is, as you might expect, flour made from finely milled oats. Note that oats are often processed in the same facility as wheat, so if you're celiac or avoiding wheat or gluten, be sure to buy oats that are certified gluten-free.

Oats (steel cut): These oats are made from whole-grain oat groats that have been cut into pieces. Like rolled oats, steel-cut oats are often processed in the same facility as wheat, so be sure to buy ones that are certified gluten-free if you're avoiding wheat or gluten.

Potato starch: This starch is made from dehydrated, peeled potatoes and is not the same as potato flour! We use potato starch in our Gluten-Free Flour Mix (page 179) because it has a neutral flavor and fine texture.

Quinoa & quinoa flour: This tiny grain is celebrated (we're talking a real party here) for its nutritional profile (it contains all essential amino acids, so it's considered a complete protein) and how quickly it cooks up (15 to 20 minutes). Quinoa flour is simply uncooked quinoa that has been finely ground. It works wonders in gluten-free baking because it provides a slightly nutty flavor and light texture.

Quinoa (puffed): Similar to other grains like rice and corn, quinoa can be popped or puffed to lighten its texture. It makes a great addition to the Superfood Salad Booster on page 169. It's not always easy to find, but its usual habitat is the cereal aisle of bulk and health food stores.

Spelt flour: This whole-grain flour is similar to wheat but has a nutty, slightly sweet flavor and lower gluten content. We love using it to make wholesome breads, muffins, and cookies.

Tapioca flour: Tapioca flour, also known as tapioca starch, is gluten-free flour derived from cassava root. It is a starchy, slightly sweet, pure-white flour often used in gluten-free baking (and is part of our Gluten-Free Flour Mix on page 179) and for thickening puddings and sauces. Look for it at bulk and health food stores.

Whole wheat pastry flour: This whole-grain flour is much softer and more finely textured than regular whole wheat flour, and baked goods made with it will have a similar consistency to those made with white flour. If you can't find it at your local grocery store, check bulk food stores, which often carry a wider variety of flours.

SWEETENERS

Sure, white sugar is deliciously addictive, but why not expand your mind and taste buds to discover the potential of other natural sweeteners, like Medjool dates? Oh, how we love those chewy, caramel-flavored dates. While the sweeteners we use in this book are still sugar, we think they're more flavorful, a little higher in nutrition, and easier for the body to process than the standard white stuff. Make some room in your cupboard for these vegan-friendly sweeties.

Agave nectar: Although there has been debate as to the healthfulness of agave, we still use it on occasion. It's a concentrated sweetener, not a health food, after all! Its clean, neutral flavor makes it suitable for recipes where you don't want the maple or caramel undertone that comes from the other sweeteners we tend to use. Look for agave in health food stores or in the specialty food section of major grocers.

Blackstrap molasses: This thick, robust syrup is a by-product of cane sugar processing and is a surprisingly nutrient-dense ingredient (it contains a good dose of iron, calcium, potassium, and more). You've likely used it to make gingerbread cookies during the holidays, but it also adds a lovely flavor component to sauces like L. P.'s Worcestershire Sauce (page 139) and BBQ Sauce (page 140) as well as baked goods like Cinnamon Graham Crackers (page 225).

Brown rice syrup: This golden syrup is derived from cooked brown rice and barley. Its mild sweetness and thick, sticky consistency similar to honey make it ideal for granola and snack bars. We love it because it has a binding quality unlike any other sweetener.

Cane sugar: Most granulated sugar on the market today is cane sugar, but some are more processed than others. That cheap, bright white sugar you find at most grocery stores has had the nutritious molasses removed, has gone through a bleaching process, and often isn't vegan due to the animal bone char used in the filtering process, which is why we prefer to use organic and unbleached evaporated cane sugar that still contains some of the molasses and is slightly tan in color rather than pure white. Wholesome Sweeteners is our favorite brand and can be found in health food stores and the specialty food or baking section of major grocers.

Coconut sugar: This sugar is produced from the sap of cut flower buds of the coconut palm tree. It is a rich, unrefined brown sugar with a hint of caramel flavor, known to be low on the glycemic index and have a high mineral content. Because of its increasing popularity, it's becoming easier to find. We usually buy it in bulk from health food stores, but you can also find it in the specialty food section of major grocers.

Maple sugar: Hey, we're Canadian. We're required by law to use maple sugar and maple syrup as often as possible. Both, as you probably guessed, are made from the sap of the sugar maple tree. Maple sugar adds a delicious maple flavor and is an excellent alternative to syrup. Depending on where you live, it may be hard to come by, but start by looking at bulk or health food stores or order some online. You may want to sing "O Canada" as you eat it.

Maple syrup: One of our favorite ways to sweeten dishes and desserts, this delicious syrup is what you get when you boil the maple tree sap to concentrate it. Maple syrup is typically graded A or B, or light or medium, but either will work in these recipes. Just be sure to use 100 percent pure maple syrup (organic preferred) and not the stuff from Aunt Jemima.

We realize it may be expensive depending on your location, but we think it's well worth the investment as a natural and less-processed sweetener.

Vanilla sugar: This flavored sugar can be found in little packets at the grocery store, but we much prefer to make it at home using unbleached cane sugar and real vanilla bean. Check out the easy recipe on page 193.

DRIED FRUIT

We use a variety of dried fruit in these recipes, from goji berries and dried figs to dried cranberries, apricots, and raisins. The only thing we suggest is to use organically grown and unsulfured dried fruit that has no sugar added, which can be found at health food stores or sometimes the specialty food section of major grocers. In a pinch, regular dried fruit is fine, too.

Medjool dates: We can't forget to mention one of our favorite natural sweeteners. Dates were crowned the fruit of the kings when they were first discovered around 6000 BC, and we understand why. This larger, sweeter variety of dates has a deep caramel flavor and can be used whole or made into Date Paste (see page 195). We often use them in no-bake desserts like the Almond Press-In Pie Crust (page 199). You can find Medjool dates in bulk and at major grocers and health food stores.

CHOCOLATE

Ah, chocolate, the one ingredient that lifts us up when we are down. You can always find some chocolate in our pantries in one form or another.

Cacao butter: Cacao butter is the pale yellow fat extracted from cacao beans. We use raw cacao butter that has not been heat processed or treated with chemicals and buy it in bulk from reputable online stores. You can also find it at some health food stores. It's well worth the investment!

Cacao nibs: Known as nature's chocolate chips, cacao nibs are made from cacao beans that have been roasted, hulled, and crumbled into

small pieces. We love using them as a garnish or to add crunch to recipes, like our Go Anywhere Chia Cereal (page 76). You can find cacao nibs at most health food stores.

Cocoa powder: For these recipes, we use natural, unsweetened cocoa powder, which doesn't contain any additives. It has a bitter taste on its own yet lends a rich, deep chocolate flavor to baked goods. Don't confuse natural cocoa powder with Dutch-process cocoa powder, which has been treated with an alkalizing agent. And make sure you don't accidentally pick up "instant cocoa" or drinking cocoa, which isn't the same thing at all—it's a mix of cocoa powder, sugar, and often dried milk, ready to be made into a cup of hot cocoa.

Dark chocolate bars/chips: We think it's worth paying a little more for good-quality dark chocolate that contains at least 70 percent cocoa, which means there is less room for fillers like milk powder and refined sugar (more fillers and sweeteners mean less of the good stuff). Always check the ingredient label to make sure it doesn't contain dairy. If you have a gluten or nut sensitivity, check to make sure the chocolate has been made in a dedicated facility. Enjoy Life and Camino are two of our favorite brands.

HERBS & SPICES

We use a variety of herbs and spices in this book. As you build your collection, don't waste your money on spices in expensive glass jars from the grocery store. Instead, find a reliable source for bulk herbs and spices and buy them in amounts according to quantities you need and will actually use. Dried herbs and spices should be replaced every six months or so anyway, so go ahead and throw out that five-year-old jug of dried basil—the flavor just won't be there anymore and it can make your food taste dull. Fresh herbs, of course, should be used within a day or two of buying them.

Black salt: Otherwise known as *kala namak*, this type of rock salt is a fabulous flavor enhancer in vegan dishes made to mimic the taste of eggs, since it provides a pronounced sulphur taste and aroma. Despite its name, *kala namak* is actually light pink in color (a little baffling, we know!). You can find it at Indian markets or specialty spice stores.

Madras masala spice blend: To save money, we sometimes use good-quality, premade Indian spice blends like Madras masala, which contains a number of intoxicating spices to create a South Indian curry mix. We love to support our favorite local spice company, Arvinda's, for this particular blend but any similar blend will do.

Vanilla beans: There is nothing like the flavor and aroma of a whole vanilla bean, which is the fruit of the vanilla orchid (indigenous to South and Central America). Be sure to purchase soft, fresh vanilla beans and use them as soon as possible. Many of our recipes call for the seeds of a vanilla bean: simply use a paring knife to split the pod down the center lengthwise and gently scrape the tiny seeds out of the inside using the dull side of your knife, then add the seeds to the recipe. You can find vanilla beans at bulk and health food stores (sometimes they come in little glass tubes).

Vanilla powder: Wait—you can get vanilla in powdered form? Yup. Once we discovered this, it became one of our favorite ways to enjoy this flavor. It's made from grinding whole vanilla beans. It can be pricey, but well worth the investment if you want to add real vanilla flavor to your desserts. We buy it from health food stores or online.

Other dried herbs and spices we use: garlic powder and garlic granules, onion powder and onion flakes, fine sea salt, ground cinnamon, ground ginger, star anise, ground cardamom, ground cloves, ground allspice, ground nutmeg, cayenne pepper, ground cumin, cumin seeds, curry powder, coriander seeds, garam masala, mustard powder, mustard seed, sweet paprika, smoked paprika, red pepper flakes, freshly ground black pepper, ground white pepper, turmeric powder, chili powder, chipotle powder, dill seed, dried dill weed, dried basil, dried thyme, dried rosemary, dried marjoram, and dried oregano.

NUTS & SEEDS

Raw nuts and seeds are staples in our kitchens since we use them as a base in many of our recipes, or for added bulk and nutrition in trail mix and granola.

In general, nuts and seeds should be stored in the fridge or freezer, especially if you live in a warmer environment and you're not going to use them right away.

Chia seeds & meal: Chia seeds are all the rage these days because of their health benefits and unique gelling action. Many people use chia meal (ground chia seeds) as a vegan egg replacer in baking or to thicken puddings and jams. You can find black and white varieties at bulk and health food stores.

Flax seeds & meal: This nutritious seed is similar to chia with its gelling power and is often used as a vegan egg replacer in baking and to add bulk and nutrition to dishes. To make flax meal, the seeds are ground to a fine powder. We prefer to grind our own (this takes seconds in a blender or coffee grinder) on an as-needed basis since the meal can go rancid after a while. Whole flaxseeds are widely available at most major grocers, and bulk and health food stores.

Hemp hearts: These hulled hemp seeds are known to be an excellent source for complete protein and balanced essential fatty acids. As you may have guessed, they come from the cannabis plant, but they are produced so the THC content is removed. We love adding them to our cereal mixes or snack bars. Hemp hearts can be found at major grocers and health food stores.

Tahini: This paste is made from raw or roasted sesame seeds and can easily be made in your own kitchen (see page 128). Tahini is used in traditional hummus recipes but also makes a delicious base for sauces and salad dressings. You can find premade tahini in the international section of grocery stores.

Other nutritious nuts and seeds we use: almonds, cashews, hazelnuts, pecans, walnuts, Brazil nuts, peanuts, sunflower seeds, sesame seeds, and pumpkin seeds.

OILS & FATS

Generally, cold-pressed, extra-virgin coconut oil is our favorite for cooking and baking, but here are a few others that are worth a place in your pantry.

SOAKING NUTS
(AN ESSENTIAL STEP)

We do a lot of soaking around here, so don't be intimidated by recipes that call for this step. Many vegan cooks we know always have a cup of cashews soaking, so if you follow their lead you can whip up something creamy any night of the week. It's super easy: just place the desired amount of cashews in a bowl and add enough water to cover them by an inch or two, cover the bowl with a lid, and let sit on your kitchen counter. We suggest soaking cashews for at least six hours, but they can be left overnight or for up to two days if refrigerated. For almonds, we suggest soaking them for at least eight hours. Drain and rinse well before using.

If you are a lucky owner of a high-speed blender like a Blendtec or Vitamix, it will take no time at all to blend the soaked nuts into a creamy, smooth consistency, but any old blender should be able to do the trick. To test for smoothness, rub the cream between your fingers—you should not feel any grittiness. If needed, give them another blend. The amount of time it takes really depends on the power of your blender and the amount of liquid used. Some recipes, particularly those for our vegan cheeses, include only a small amount of liquid in order to get firm results, so take care to follow the instructions as best you can and only add more liquid a little at a time if absolutely necessary. Some blenders are a little needy. But hey, who are we to judge?

Canola oil: Very mild in flavor, canola oil is our preferred choice in recipes when a neutral-tasting oil is desired, but you can substitute another mild oil like sunflower or grapeseed, if you wish. Most canola crops are genetically modified—if this is a concern, choose certified organic brands.

Coconut butter: Made from whole coconut flesh (not just the oil), coconut butter is a dense spread with a rich, buttery flavor. We love using it to make frostings and fillings, or to add a little softness to chocolate coatings. We tell you the secret to making your own on page 112, but you can also find premade coconut butter at health food stores.

Coconut oil: Coconut oil is the edible oil extracted from mature coconuts. We always use cold-pressed, organic, extra-virgin oil, which means the oil has not been refined, bleached, or deodorized. With its high smoke point, coconut oil is great for high-heat cooking without damaging the properties of the oil. Solid at room temperature up to 75°F, it also makes a great replacement for butter in many recipes and helps raw recipes maintain a solid texture. If you don't like the taste of coconut, you can always get refined coconut oil, which is mellower in flavor. These days, coconut oil is easy to find at most major grocers and health food stores.

Olive oil: This rich, earthy, and fruity-flavored oil has its place in every kitchen. We use small amounts of cold-pressed, organic, extra-virgin olive oil for sauces and dressings, and to add a little crispness to baked chips.

Sesame oil: We use this oil on occasion because it adds a lovely fragrant sesame taste to finished dishes, sauces, and dressings. Toasted sesame oil has a more intense flavor compared to the regular stuff, so just a little goes a long way.

SEA VEGETABLES

Agar: This magical ingredient made from seaweed is used as a vegan substitute for gelatin. You'll find Nicole forever talking about the wonders of agar and how, when dissolved in boiling liquid, it magically transforms into something incredible, like the Buffalo Mozzarella on page 54. Purchase agar in either flaked or powdered form from well-stocked health food stores, Asian markets, or online. Our favorite brands are Eden Organic (for flakes) and NOW Real Food (for powder).

Kelp: Kelp is seaweed commonly used in Asian cuisine, but it is also a secret staple for veganizing dishes where we want to omit fish- or shrimp-derived ingredients. Whether you're making vegan-friendly soup, mock tuna salad, sushi, or salad dressing, this ingredient will provide a subtly salty, umami-rich flavor. Although kelp evokes the ocean, it is not overwhelming, and many people simply use it as a salt substitute. Kelp granules can be found in most health food stores near the nori or in the salt aisle of Asian markets.

GUMS & EMULSIFIERS

These ingredients may not be familiar to you, but they work magic in some of our recipes, binding, thickening, and creating volume. Just a little goes a long way.

Lecithin: This is an indispensable recipe helper that is used as an emulsifier to bind ingredients that wouldn't normally mix together, like oil and water. We use it to create stable salad dressings, dairy-free butter, and coffee creamer. Made from soybeans or sunflower seeds, lecithin can be found in both liquid and granule forms from the supplement section of health food stores and some grocery stores.

Xanthan gum: Bet you never thought you'd be buying ingredients that started with the letter X. Don't let the weird name scare you—this is great for thickening liquids or adding volume and creaminess. In gluten-free baking, we can nearly replicate the stretching and structural characteristics of gluten if we add a little xanthan to the recipe. It's a fine white powder that can be found in the baking aisle of bulk and health food stores. Don't worry, you don't have to know how to pronounce it.

SOY PRODUCTS

Bragg Liquid Aminos: This salty liquid condiment is a protein concentrate derived from soybeans and is similar to soy sauce, tamari, and nama shoyu. It's high in a number of essential and nonessential amino acids. We love using it to add that umami boost to sauces, dressings, and stir-frys. Look for it at health food stores or the specialty food section of major grocers.

Miso: We use this fermented Japanese paste to flavor many dishes, and it is particularly useful for homemade cheese. The standard kind is made from soybeans, but there are dozens of varieties out there (brown rice, chickpea, barley), which can be found at health food stores, Asian markets, or some large grocers that have a good international section. The recipes in this book use white miso, which is lighter in color and has a mild, slightly sweet flavor, or brown rice miso, which is dark in color, and rich and full bodied in flavor.

Tamari: Similar to soy sauce and Bragg Liquid Aminos, tamari is made from fermented soybeans with little or no wheat, so it's a great gluten-free alternative. The good Japanese varieties are smoother and more complex in flavor than soy sauce, so it has become our go-to for sauces and dressings like the Sweet Ginger Stir-Fry Sauce on page 132.

VINEGARS & WINES

Apple cider vinegar: Another staple in our kitchens, apple cider vinegar is made from—you guessed it—apples. We prefer to use organic, unpasteurized brands like Bragg or Eden Organic to add a little tang to salad dressings, to help baked goods rise, and, because it's antibacterial and environmentally friendly, to clean our homes!

Mirin: A rice wine similar to sake but with a lower alcohol content, mirin is a staple in Japanese cuisine and is used for, among other things, teriyaki sauce, sushi rice, and marinades. We use it in the Sweet Ginger Stir-Fry Sauce on page 132.

Rice vinegar: A sweeter, more delicate alternative to distilled white vinegar, rice vinegar is made from fermented rice or rice wine. We love the unseasoned variety for stir-fry dishes and to add the sour to the Sweet & Sour Dipping Sauce on page 137.

OTHER VEGAN ESSENTIALS

While these ingredients don't really fit into any of the other categories, we still consider them super useful.

Capers: These small green herb buds have long been a favorite in the Mediterranean region. They are dried and then brined or packed in salt. Because they are cured like olives, they lend a piquant sour and salty flavor to salads, dressings, and sauces. For these recipes, we use the brined variety found in the jarred olives section of grocery stores.

Carob chips: An excellent low-sugar alternative to chocolate, carob is made from the fruit of the carob plant, which grows along the Mediterranean Sea. Carob chips look just like chocolate chips, although the flavor is more mellow and earthier than chocolate. We love them as a topping for the Awesome Energy Bars on page 89.

Citric acid: This natural acid is very bitter and gives fruits like lemons and limes their characteristic sour flavor. It's sometimes used as a preservative, but a small amount can also boost the tanginess of dishes. Citric acid is commonly sold as a white powder and can be found in the baking or candy-making aisle of large grocers or bulk food stores.

Coconut milk: Canned coconut milk adds a rich, creamy quality that mimics dairy cream in recipes. Throughout this book, we use full-fat coconut milk, not "lite." The percentage of fat can vary by brand, so look for brands with at least 16 percent fat (you'll find this info on the nutrition facts label). Our preferred brands are Thai Kitchen or Native Forest. Thai Kitchen, however, doesn't separate well, so for recipes that require chilling overnight to separate the cream from the water (required for the Coconut Yogurt on page 45), we find organic brands like Native Forest work best.

Liquid smoke: This potent, concentrated seasoning adds a smoky, hickory, mesquite flavor to recipes like the Coconut Bacon Bits on page 101. It's made by burning wood chips and reducing the concentrated smoke into liquid. This seasoning can be found in the BBQ sauce section of many grocery stores.

Maca powder: This root vegetable has a long history as a superfood. It is also known to add a distinct malty flavor and is often paired with chocolate, but we like to use it to intensify the flavor of cheesy dishes like the Mac & Cheese Sauce Mix on page 159. Look for maca powder at health and bulk food stores.

Nutritional yeast: If you don't already have a bag of nutritional yeast in your pantry, go out and buy some immediately! Lovingly known as nooch by those who use it regularly, this deactivated yeast adds a cheesy flavor in vegan recipes and is an essential component to some of our recipes, like Mac & Cheese Sauce Mix (page 159) and Nacho Cheese Sauce (page 136). We buy it in flaked form from bulk and health food stores; it is also available in larger grocery stores.

Probiotic: This digestive supplement is used to add the authentic fermented tang to our vegan cheeses. There are quite a few vegan probiotic brands on the market that come in capsule or powdered form. We like both Trophic and NuChapter. If you pick up your probiotic in capsule form, just make sure it is gelatin-free. Usually it says "veg-capsule" or "vegan" right on the label.

Psyllium husks: Another weird name, but you'll want to get to know these plants because psyllium husks provide fiber that expands and forms a gel-like texture when added to liquid. They are often used as a binder in vegan and gluten-free baking. Psyllium is available as a powder and as whole husks at health and bulk food stores—we use the whole husks in our recipes.

Yeast (fast rising dry): Also known as rapid-rise or quick-rise yeast, this active yeast is milled into smaller particles so it doesn't need to be dissolved in water like traditional bread yeast. Do not substitute for traditional active dry yeast or bread machine yeast. Fleischmann's is a good and commonly available brand. Be sure to check the expiry date to ensure it's still active.

STORING YOUR HOMEMADE STAPLES

In every recipe, we offer guidelines and suggestions on how best to store the goods. In most cases, the fridge or freezer is your best friend and will keep your precious homemade staples from going bad too fast.

If you plan to use that pancake mix or buckwheat cereal within a couple of weeks or so, then storing it at room temp is fine. But for longer storing, the freezer is likely a good place for it to go. All of the mixes in the book, plus most desserts and snacks, can be frozen in freezer bags or freezer-safe containers for a few months.

Recipes that involve nuts and seeds should also be stored in a cold environment to keep them from going rancid over time.

If you like to be extra conscious, it's also a good idea to label your homemade staples with the date you made them so you don't have to question how long they've been there when you go to use them. If you've ever found a mystery bag of something at the bottom of your freezer, you'll know what we mean.

A NOTE ABOUT HOMEMADE INGREDIENTS

Many recipes in this book make use of ingredients you can also make yourself. If a recipe calls for almond milk, for example, you can make it in your own kitchen using the Basic Nut/Seed Milk on page 37, or if it calls for almond butter you can use the recipe for Basic Nut Butter on page 106, or for pure vanilla extract, try the recipe on page 192. Similarly, any recipe that calls for flour like oat or buckwheat can be homemade following the recipe for Basic Fresh Flours on page 190. Of course, the store-bought stuff is just fine, too! Don't feel that your salad dressing, granola bars, or cookie mix is any less homemade if you use store-bought almond milk, almond butter, vanilla extract, or flour.

Not everyone has time to make everything from scratch. We get it. But the option is there if you want it or already have a specific homemade ingredient on hand.

MAKE IT GLUTEN-FREE

While many of the things we make at home are naturally gluten-free, there are some recipes that taste delightful using whole wheat or spelt flour, like the Chocolate Cake Mix on page 183 or the Premade Pie Crust on page 202. In these instances, we've also included gluten-free substitution options (called "Make it gluten-free") at the bottom of the recipes. That way, no matter if you live a gluten-free or gluten-friendly life, you can enjoy every recipe in this book.

CHAPTER 2

Equipment Essentials and Techniques

· ·

IF YOU'RE A NOVICE COOK, or new to setting up a vegan kitchen, this chapter will be a valuable resource. Over the years, we've figured out the tools and gadgets that work best for us. We favor ones that make our time in the kitchen more efficient and more fun, and that don't take up too much space. We love multitaskers and versatile equipment—basically, we like a sous chef that we can plug in or turn off. Your favorite tools will depend on the recipes you make regularly and the skills you feel a machine does better. To get you started, we've included an overview below of the equipment we rely on daily in our kitchens and for all the recipes in this book.

Blender: With the smoothie revolution, blenders have seen a significant resurgence in recent years. Once relegated to the back of a cupboard, blenders now seem to have secured their spot as a countertop essential. Blenders are designed to liquefy, but that doesn't mean you can only make liquids. They are a versatile tool we depend on. If you're simply making smoothies and sauces, there are a lot of great, affordable blenders that can do the job. But you'll see throughout this book that we turn to our blenders for a whole lot more than liquefying fruit, which has led us to rely on multitasking superstar Blendtec. It isn't a quiet blender but it can easily churn up a cheesecake batter, blitz oats into a quick flour, or turn tomatoes into a silky smooth sauce.

> The easiest way to clean your blender is to fill it about a third of the way with water and add a couple drops of dish detergent. Pulse to swirl around the suds. Pour out the mixture and rinse thoroughly.

Citrus reamer/hand juicer: Fresh citrus juice is a culinary game changer. To make it easier to infuse your recipes with these bright, bold flavors, a handheld citrus reamer (usually made from metal or wood) or a small hand juicer (which looks like a citrus reamer secured to the top of a small container that holds the juice) is ideal. Both are easy to find and inexpensive.

> If you get into the habit of using fresh citrus, it is an amazing time-saver to juice a batch of lemons and limes once a week and store the juice in jars in the fridge to have on hand and ready for recipes.

Cooling rack: A wire cooling rack is a common tool for bakers. When cookies, breads, or pastries are pulled from the oven and transferred to a cooling rack on the counter, it provides just enough space underneath the confections for air to circulate and for the treats to cool evenly. But that's not all it can do. With parchment paper placed underneath, a cooling rack makes a great garnishing station. Just imagine how much easier it is to evenly drizzle chocolate over a tray of snack bars, and then pull away the parchment from underneath and place the whole cooling rack in the fridge for the chocolate to firm. Air-aged cheeses also benefit from a cooling rack. As with the warm treats mentioned above, the cooling rack lets the air circulate around the cheese, allowing a rind to form and the cheese to firm evenly.

Food processor: The best sous chef we've ever had is the food processor. This is the magic machine that can make butter from nuts, turn bananas into ice cream, and make the most incredible hummus we've ever tasted. Unlike a blender, which tries to make everything into a liquid, a food processor is designed to grind or chop. It won't seize up from lack of liquid like a blender will; instead, it makes steady work of breaking things down. Cuisinart is our brand of choice because they seem to last forever. Depending on the number of people in your household or how much batch cooking you do, try to work with the smallest bowl size that will accommodate the recipe. The contents need to have lots of contact with the blades for the food processor to do its work, so if you add just a couple of almonds, they will bounce around, avoiding the blade, but add a couple of handfuls and you're in business.

Many food processors come with other attachments, including ones for slicing vegetables, which can save you lots of time when preparing salads and slaws—and will contain the stain of beet juice. A plastic S-blade is a great attachment to use for kneading dough for breads and pizzas.

Kitchen scale: In Canada and the United States, we tend toward cups, teaspoons, and tablespoons to measure out our recipes, while in the United Kingdom, Australia, and other areas, the kitchen scale is king. Although we agree that a kitchen scale ensures more reliable results as the size of cups can vary and some ingredients are just hard to fit into a measuring cup for an accurate measurement, we know it is a cooking style few in North America have adopted. However, we find a kitchen scale is the ideal way to measure chocolate, which is often listed in recipes by the number of ounces.

Mandoline: Most home cooks do not have the knife skills of a sushi master—meaning paper-thin slices can be difficult to produce and time-consuming to create. So, we recommend a mandoline or V-slicer, which turns that laborious process into a two-second task. A mandoline has a very sharp blade inserted into a piece of metal or plastic. The thickness of the desired slice can be adjusted using a dial. Then grasping the vegetable you need to slice in one hand (wearing a hand guard) and holding the mandoline with the other, you run the vegetable across the blade with even force in a fluid motion. The perfect slices slip out the underside of the blade as you go. A V-slicer is similar but has only a standard set of thicknesses available and is adjusted by changing the blades for the thickness required. For recipes where thickness matters, a mandoline or V-slicer is an incredible tool—think crispy, crunchy sweet potato chips in particular.

Mason jars: Our entire pantries are contained in mason jars. Mason jars are endlessly reusable, available in a myriad of sizes, and easy to stack, store, and transport. Glass jars with a screw-on lid keep dry ingredients fresh longer, can be used to shake up salad dressing and sauces stored in the fridge, and can become the most versatile lunchbox you've ever owned. Mason jars can go from microwave to fridge to freezer to dishwasher, which makes them the go-to container in our kitchens. We like to pick them up from grocery stores or hardware stores at the end of the summer when the time for preserving the harvest makes them readily available.

Measuring cups: If nothing else, your kitchen needs measuring cups. Making recipes reliable all comes down to ratios. For better results, we recommend using dry measuring cups (the ones you often see stacked inside each other) for dry ingredients and liquid measuring cups (usually plastic or glass, with a spouted edge and the amounts written up the side) for liquids.

Nut milk bag: This could be the punchline to some X-rated jokes, but in our context it's just a thin cloth bag with a drawstring top. It is used to make nut milks and cheeses because the weave is fine enough to let just the liquid through, retaining the pulp or cheese base, for a super-smooth result. Although cheesecloth can be used as an alternative, it is a bit more complicated, as you need to layer pieces of cloth to get the right weave for straining. As nut milk bags can be tossed in the washing machine to be ready for their next use, they are a practical, eco-friendly investment. Nut milk bags are becoming increasingly popular and can be found in many health food stores and online at very reasonable prices.

Offset spatula: Lisa's very favorite kitchen utensil. An offset spatula looks a little like a knife that is bent in the middle. It is an amazing tool for spreading frostings and chocolate, scraping down the sides of blenders and food processors, and any general smoothing tasks in your kitchen. Affordable and versatile, it gets an A+ from us.

Pizza cutter: Although typically used for rolling across saucy pies to slice a circle into perfect wedges, the pizza cutter can do so much more. The thin blade makes it ideal for precise cuts, and the ease of rolling it makes quick work of cutting a big batch of crackers into perfect diamonds.

Sieve: Sieves are available in a vast variety of shapes and sizes. For most of the recipes in this book, we use a fine-mesh metal sieve to drain the liquid. The fine weave makes sure we don't lose anything unintentionally, and the metal is easy to clean. Our metal sieve is an essential part of the cheese-making process.

Silpat baking mat: Although many of our recipes call for parchment paper–lined baking sheets, our preference is always to use something reusable, which is where Silpat comes in. A Silpat is a silicone-based baking mat you can place on top of your baking pan to make sure there is no sticking or scraping. Silpat is easily washed with a gentle scrub in soap and water and rolled up for its next use. We are big fans of this French invention, but there are times when we prefer parchment. The thickness and silicone texture of the Silpat can make it harder to achieve a crispy crust, so if you're looking for crunch, parchment works best.

Spice grinder: Often used by coffee lovers for a fresh daily grind, spice grinders are perfectly designed for grinding seeds and spices into fine powders. Relatively inexpensive and incredibly effective, these are a great tool for making your own fresh spice blends, powders, and pastes. We also use a spice grinder to grind vanilla beans into a fine powder for some special treats.

> Getting rid of the coffee taste—if you already use a spice grinder for your daily java but want to start creating your own spice blends, you don't need to get a second grinder. Instead, run a handful of dry white rice through the grinder to absorb all of the coffee flavor before starting to grind your spices. Discard the rice, remove any residue with a dry cloth or paper towel, and you're ready to toss together your favorite whole spices.

Stand mixer: You might think you don't need a stand mixer. But imagine this: you start the process, and the machine whips up the coconut cream while you casually steep yourself a cup of tea and sip it while browsing through a magazine. Oh, look, the cream is all whipped. Wasn't that easy? A stand mixer can be a powerhouse in your kitchen. It can provide the muscle for recipes that require extended whipping, kneading, or mixing. Although not required for many of the recipes in this book, a stand mixer can save you time and improve the reliability of your recipe results. We use our mixer for recipes like whipped cream, frosting, pizza dough, and bread.

Thermometer: We use a couple of different types of thermometers in this book, but the one we recommend most strongly is the oven thermometer. Everyone assumes that turning your oven to 350°F means it will heat to 350°F, but the surprising thing is that most ovens are a little bit off, and they can become more so over time. A cheap investment with reliable results, an oven thermometer is hung from an oven rack and will tell you precisely the temperature your oven reaches. With ingredients like coconut flakes and seeds, a few degrees can mean the difference between terrifically toasty and charred beyond recognition.

Whisk: Why stir when you can whisk? The whisk is a great tool for bringing liquids together. It has an amazing ability to emulsify and adds air as you stir. Readily available and affordable, every kitchen should have a whisk.

Zester: Another citrus ambassador, the zester makes it easy to infuse recipes with bright flavor without adding additional liquid. There are many different types of zesters available. We prefer to use a Microplane-style zester as it makes a very fine zest, which enhances recipes without changing their texture. Microplanes are chef makers—for some reason, topping off a dish with a fine sprinkle of citrus zest makes us all feel like we deserve a series on the Food Network. On our show, we won't stop at citrus—we'll use that Microplane to grate ginger, garlic, nutmeg, and chocolate. (But we'll never say "BAM.")

TECHNIQUES AND TROUBLESHOOTING

THE SECRET TO ROLLING DOUGH FOR PASTRY, COOKIES, AND CRACKERS

We once had a pretty rocky relationship with dough that required rolling. Pie crusts, cookies, and crackers—we love them, for sure, but rolling out the dough was beyond intimidating. So we did what most people would do: we avoided making them. That is, until we gained confidence—by making pie dough over and over and over, making mistakes, fixing those mistakes, and remembering not to make the same mistakes the next time around. Messy, flour-covered countertops and sticky rolling pins, no more! The know-how is what we're here for.

1. Use natural, unbleached parchment baking paper (it's lighter and less stiff and slippery than standard baking paper or waxed paper) to roll out the dough.

2. Cut two pieces of parchment that are large enough to cover the surface of the rolled-out dough (generally about 12 x 16 inches for these recipes; if you can find the precut parchment sheets, even better).

3. Place one piece of parchment on your countertop with one long side facing you. Place the mound of dough on the parchment and shape it into a disc with your hands. Place another piece of parchment on top. Take the edges of the two pieces of parchment closest to you and slip them over the lip of your countertop. Press your abdomen against it to hold it tight against the counter while you grab your rolling pin and begin to roll. This keeps the paper in place so it doesn't move around the counter as you roll.

4. Roll from the center out, using a steady, even pressure. As you roll out the dough, rotate the paper (again, holding the edge closest to you against your abs) so you roll in even directions to produce an even shape (as directed in the recipe). Release the paper, rotate, and hold again.

5. Occasionally lift the top piece of parchment if you find it folding into the dough and creating creases. Check the thickness of the dough as directed in the recipe.

6. If transferring the dough to a pie plate or baking sheet, simply slide the palm of your hand underneath the dough on the parchment and flip it into your pie plate, removing the parchment paper, or slide it directly onto the baking sheet leaving the parchment underneath.

HOW TO CULTURE NUT CHEESES WITH CHEESECLOTH OR A NUT MILK BAG

Cheese-making is a process, but with a little investment of time (and cashews) you'll be turning out incredible, artisan-style nut cheese, customized to your tastes, regularly and reliably.

1. Soak your nuts for the full amount of time listed in the recipe (6 or 8 hours). Softer nuts are easier to blend.

2. Set up your culturing station. Grab your fine-mesh metal sieve and find a bowl that it fits perfectly inside. The sieve should rest on the lip of the bowl, but the bottom of the sieve should not touch the bottom of the bowl.

Classic Cheese Ball (page 60)

3. Line the sieve with a nut milk bag or two or three pieces of cheese-cloth. The cheesecloth should be layered (in a crisscross fashion) to make the holes in the cloth as small as possible.

4. Blend the cheese mixture and pour it into the nut milk bag or cheese-cloth. Pull the nut milk bag closed or wrap the cheesecloth over the top of the cheese. Place a weight on top, like a soup can or a jar of coconut oil, to press out the water. It should apply gentle pressure, so be conscious of the amount of weight you choose to add.

5. If you're making cheese in a warm climate, fermenting on your countertop will probably work just fine; if it is colder where you live, try fermenting the cheese in the oven with just the light on, or on top of your refrigerator.

6. Ferment the cheese, following the time suggested in the recipe.

7. Once fermented, discard any liquid that was released by the cheese. Scrape the cheese into the bowl from the nut milk bag (turning it inside out helps) or the cheesecloth. Add any additional ingredients and stir to combine. Thoroughly rinse out your nut milk bag and give it a good wash, or discard the cheesecloth.

8. If you're creating a firm, sliceable cheese, transfer it to a ring mold and place it in the freezer to firm. Once firm enough, remove the cheese from the mold, coat your hands in salt, and gently rub the sides of the cheese.

9. For air-drying, place the cheese on a cooling rack on your counter and follow the time guidelines in the recipe. If you live in a warm environment, it might help to place the cheese on a piece of parchment paper on top of a cooling rack (to prevent the cheese from melting through). If using parchment, you'll need to flip it over after it has firmed up and started to develop a rind on top. Discard the parchment and let the cheese air-dry until it develops a rind on the underside and becomes firm enough to slice.

10. Once finished fermenting, the cheese can be stored in the fridge or freezer for an extended period of time—up to a month in the fridge or several months in the freezer.

WHAT IF . . . ? MORE QUESTIONS AND ANSWERS ABOUT MAKING VEGAN CHEESES

1. I've added all the water the recipe called for, but my cheese is still chunky/gritty.

In cheese-making, smoothness is paramount. If your blender is struggling to produce a silky-smooth result, we suggest grinding the nuts in a dry blender before adding the liquid. Grind the nuts into a fine meal or flour. Add the liquid a little at a time, scraping down the sides between each addition, to allow time for the blender to work on incorporating the liquid and further breaking down the nuts. As a very last result, add a teaspoon more liquid. But patience often works better in the end than the addition of extra liquid.

2. I added more water than the recipe called for and my cheese is too soft.

When you set up the cheese to ferment, add a little extra weight to see if you can get some of the excess liquid out of the cheese before you attempt to shape it.

If you have a dehydrator, it can work magic on soft cheeses. Place the cheese in a ring mold in the dehydrator and dehydrate at 110°F for 24 hours. Release the cheese from the mold, flip it over to dry out the underside, and dehydrate for 4 to 6 hours more.

If you do not have a dehydrator, transfer the cheese as best you can onto a small piece of parchment paper. Shape it into a round. Sprinkle the top and sides with salt, and allow to air-dry according to the recipe instructions. If after air-drying it is still too soft to slice, store it in the freezer and slice while frozen, or shape it into a log and wrap in plastic wrap to keep in the fridge for spreading and slicing.

3. I made a beautiful cheese, but it is too sour for my taste.

This time around, serve it up with something sweet, like Strawberry Chia Jam (page 111). But make a note for next time. The best part about making your own cheese at home is being able to customize the flavor to your taste. If it is too sour, it may be that the amount of culturing time in the recipe is too long for your flavor preference. Try reducing the air-drying time by 12 hours to see if that takes off the edge. If the result is still too sour, reduce the amount of lemon juice in the recipe by one-third.

4. I'm allergic to cashews. Is cheese-making out of the question for me?

Absolutely not. Vegan cheese can be made from a variety of ingredients. If you are allergic to cashews, try macadamia nuts instead. They produce a firmer cheese and may require just a touch more liquid to achieve a creamy result. Cheese can also be made from almonds, sunflower seeds, Brazil nuts, and hemp hearts. Experiment with different combinations until you discover the perfect cheese for you.

5. I'm ready to get fancier with my cheese-making. How do I create a beautiful cheese plate to serve my guests?

First, decide if you're setting up a sweet or savory cheese plate. Sweet is ideal for after dinner, while savory makes for a wonderful appetizer course.

For a sweet plate:

- Pick out three to five sweet and creamy cheeses, such as Cultured Nut Cheese (rolled in dried fruit and chopped nuts; page 49), Date and Fig Cashew Cheese (page 58), and Cheddar Cheese (page 52). Set out a small knife beside each type of cheese.
- Add dried fruits like cherries, figs, or cranberries and fresh fruits like grapes, berries, and apples to start to fill the plate. A few small handfuls of lightly toasted nuts is another great addition.
- To complete the plate, consider the addition of sweet preserves or spreads, such as berry jams or fruit preserves, crackers (especially the Pecan and Raisin Rice Crackers on page 96), and a sliced baguette.

For a savory plate:

- Pick out three to five savory or spicy cheeses, such as the Classic Cheese Ball (page 60), Spicy Jalapeño Cheese (page 56), and Buffalo Mozzarella (page 54). Set out a small knife beside each type of cheese.
- Add smoked or marinated olives, sun-dried tomatoes, or roasted bell peppers or zucchini to start to create a party platter. Roasted tamari almonds are a wonderful addition.
- Finish the plate with some crunchy, seedy crackers, a firm rye or pumpernickel bread, or a firm, crusty baguette.

• •

HOW TO MELT CHOCOLATE IN A DOUBLE BOILER

If you don't own an actual double boiler, you can use this method to make sure your chocolate melts slowly, evenly, and without any grittiness.

1. Fill a small saucepan two-thirds full with water.
2. Find a small heatproof bowl (stainless steel or glass works well) that fits tightly over the saucepan with just enough space that the bottom of the bowl does not touch the water in the pan (if it does, pour out some water).
3. Chop the amount of chocolate called for in the recipe into small chunks (about the size of chocolate chips). A chef's knife works well for chopping chocolate. If you're using chocolate chips for the recipe, measure the amount needed.
4. Place the chocolate into the heatproof bowl, place the bowl over the saucepan, and set the saucepan over medium-low heat. Once the water comes to a simmer, reduce the heat to low.
5. Allow the chocolate to melt without stirring until at least three-quarters of the chocolate has turned into a liquid. Remove the bowl from the saucepan and gently stir the chocolate to melt the remaining chunks.
6. If the chocolate cools too quickly and begins to firm, return the bowl to the saucepan and heat slowly until it melts again. If your recipe requires dipping, the melted chocolate can remain on the double boiler, with the temperature at very low, while you dip.

CHAPTER 3

DIY-ing Your Dairy-Free Staples

· ·

WHEN WE'RE STANDING IN LINE at the grocery store and we see a lovely someone in front of us stocking up on soymilk, Tofutti cream cheese, coconut milk ice cream, and nondairy cheese, first we think, "Hey, vegan!" and then we think, "Can we help you with that?"

Not the vegan part (we're pretty thrilled about that), but the weight of the whole prepackaged pile we'd like to take off their shoulders. We get busy, too, and we agree that it's amazing that you can now find soy milk at grocery stores around the world, but every package costs money for water, plastic, and shipping. We'd like to save said dollars for something more exciting, like shipping ourselves somewhere tropical!

So, in this chapter, you'll find all the solutions you need to lighten the heft of your grocery haul by whipping up everything from oat milk to cheddar cheese to frozen yogurt at home. We've got secrets for making your own fortified milk and coconut whipped cream, and creating concoctions like cookie crumbs from your magical milk leftovers. With these tricks and techniques, no matter where you live in the world, you'll have access to all the best dairy alternatives available (right in your own kitchen).

Basic Nut/Seed Milk

Soak, blend, strain! Thankfully, making your own plant-based milk is as easy as 1-2-3 and doesn't require a guy in overalls hooking up a cow to a machine. The only difficult part is remembering to soak your nuts or seeds to give them time to soften and improve digestibility (if that's too much to ask, try the Easy Almond Milk on page 38). Costly equipment isn't even required, as your old blender will do a proper job. To strain the pulp from the fresh milk, a fine-mesh sieve or cheesecloth will do the trick, but we love our reusable mesh nut milk bags, which are available for less than ten dollars at health food stores or online. They're easy to clean and less wasteful than cheesecloth. Plus, they do double duty for culturing cheese (see page 49).

You can start with a batch of almond milk to get comfortable and then play around with different combinations of nuts and seeds to find your favorite flavor—we love combining almonds, Brazil nuts, and hemp seeds, for example. You can also add flavorings like vanilla, cocoa powder, or fresh fruit (hint: strawberry-flavored milk is incredible), or spices like cinnamon or nutmeg to keep things interesting.

INGREDIENTS

1 cup raw nuts and/or seeds, soaked in water for 8 hours (note: hemp seeds don't need to be soaked)

Optional add-ins: 2 pitted Medjool dates or other sweetener to taste, ½ to 1 teaspoon pure vanilla extract to taste, pinch of ground cinnamon or nutmeg

TIP: Don't dispose of the precious pulp! Leftover pulp can be stored in a sealed container or bag in the freezer and used to make Almond Pulp Cookie Crumbs (page 223).

INSTRUCTIONS

1. Drain and rinse the nuts/seeds.
2. Using a blender, blend the nuts/seeds with 3 cups water (and add up to 1 cup more if desired to thin out; the resulting consistency will depend on how much water you choose to use) and any optional add-ins on high speed for about 1 minute, until the nuts are broken down and the liquid is fairly smooth.
3. For a silky milk consistency, strain the mixture through a nut milk bag or a few layers of cheesecloth that is held over a bowl or milk container. Squeeze gently to get all the liquid out. Store milk in a mason jar in the fridge for up to 5 days. The milk may separate while sitting, so be sure to give the jar a shake before using.

Easy Almond Milk

MAKES ABOUT 2 CUPS

Need milk in an instant? Follow this simple recipe and you'll be enjoying a perfect, sweet beverage before you know it. Using roasted almond butter results in a more flavorful and almondy milk. If you prefer something milder, try cashew butter instead.

INGREDIENTS

2 tablespoons almond or cashew butter

Optional add-ins: 1 to 2 teaspoons maple syrup or other liquid sweetener, ¼ teaspoon pure vanilla extract, pinch of ground cinnamon or freshly grated nutmeg

INSTRUCTIONS

In a blender, combine 2 cups water, the almond butter, and any optional add-ins and blend on high speed until smooth. Enjoy immediately or store in a mason jar in the fridge for up to 5 days. The milk may separate while sitting, so be sure to give the jar a shake before using.

Oat, Quinoa, or Rice Milk

MAKES ABOUT 1¼ CUPS

Sick of soy? Over almonds? Mix up your milk routine with something new.

INGREDIENTS

⅓ cup uncooked rolled oats, cooked quinoa, or cooked short-grain brown rice, cooled

1 Medjool date, pitted

Pinch of sea salt

½ teaspoon pure vanilla extract

INSTRUCTIONS

1. If making oat milk, combine the oats and 1 cup water in a blender and allow to sit for 30 minutes. If making quinoa or rice milk, combine the grain with the water and proceed immediately to Step 2.
2. Add the date, salt, and vanilla, and blend until completely smooth. Store in an airtight container in the fridge for 5 to 7 days.

TRY THIS: If you're looking for a more savory milk, replace the vanilla extract with the same amount of lemon juice.

Sweetened Condensed Milk

· ·

MAKES ABOUT 1 CUP

Here you have it—a vegan version of sweetened condensed milk. To create it, homemade cashew milk is heated to produce a slightly thicker, creamier version of itself, perfect for adding to coffee, tea, milkshakes, and desserts.

INGREDIENTS

½ cup raw cashews, soaked in water for 6 hours

3 Medjool dates, pitted

2 teaspoons cane sugar

¼ teaspoon pure vanilla extract

INSTRUCTIONS

1. Drain and rinse the soaked cashews.
2. In a blender, combine the cashews, dates, and cane sugar with 1¼ cups water and blend until the nuts are broken down and the mixture is fairly smooth.
3. Strain the mixture through a nut milk bag or a few layers of cheesecloth set in a fine-mesh sieve over a small saucepan. Squeeze gently to get all the liquid out.
4. Heat the milk in the saucepan over medium heat. As soon as it comes to a boil, reduce the heat to low and simmer, whisking frequently, for a minute or two, until thickened. Remove from the heat and whisk in the vanilla. Store in a mason jar in the fridge for up to 5 days.

Whipped Cream

. . . .

MAKES 2 CUPS

Things have been oh-so-creamy in our world ever since the discovery of full-fat coconut milk and its glorious attributes and uses, and so it made the perfect base for this heavenly whipped cream. To obtain the thick, stable quality of traditional varieties, we use a plant-based gelatin substitute called agar (see page 13). This whipped cream needs some time in the fridge after being blended into a "whip," so be sure to make this ahead—ideally, a day before you need it.

INGREDIENTS

1 (13.5-ounce) can full-fat coconut milk

2 tablespoons agar flakes, or 1¼ teaspoons agar powder

2 tablespoons pure maple syrup

¼ cup raw cashews, soaked in water for 6 hours

1 teaspoon pure vanilla extract

> **TIP:** It's important to use full-fat coconut milk (not "lite") for this recipe. A good-quality brand, like Thai Kitchen, is recommended for best consistency and flavor.

INSTRUCTIONS

1. In a small saucepan, combine the coconut milk, agar flakes, and maple syrup and whisk vigorously so there are no clumps of agar. Bring to a boil over medium heat, then reduce the heat to maintain a simmer and cook for 10 minutes. Watch carefully—if the heat is too high, the coconut milk will foam up and boil over.

2. Pour the mixture into a large metal bowl and place in the freezer for about 45 minutes just to get it very cold, but not frozen. It should feel firm to the touch and kind of rubbery.

3. Scoop the gel into a blender. Drain and rinse the cashews and add them to the blender along with the vanilla. Blend on high speed for about a minute, until very smooth (this step also incorporates the air bubbles it needs to make the cream fluffy). Return the cream to the fridge to firm up for at least 3 hours (or overnight, if you can swing it). The longer you let it set, the thicker it will become. If you own a hand mixer, feel free to use it to "whip" up the cream before serving; otherwise, just give it a good stir. Whipped cream can be stored in an airtight container in the fridge for up to 1 week.

Cashew Coffee Creamer

· ·

MAKES ABOUT 1¼ CUPS

Before dairy-free milks were conveniently found at every café counter, I took my coffee black. I didn't mind the bitter note and enjoyed how my order seemed to give me a higher status—with nods of acceptance from the barista. I felt kind of tough. And then I tried the first sweet vegan coffee creamers to hit the shelves. There was no going back to black. It seems many people, much smarter than me, already knew the transformative power of a few tablespoons of cream. Coffee became something to be enjoyed, not endured. And now you have my answer to special Saturday morning moments: cashew creamer, made at home, in your pajamas. —L. P.

INGREDIENTS

⅓ cup raw cashews, soaked in water for 6 hours

2 teaspoons soy lecithin granules or liquid sunflower lecithin

1½ tablespoons pure maple syrup

½ teaspoon pure vanilla extract

INSTRUCTIONS

1. Drain and rinse the soaked cashews.
2. In a blender, combine the cashews and ⅔ cup water and blend until very smooth.
3. Strain the cashew milk through a fine-mesh sieve lined with cheesecloth or a nut milk bag. Return the strained milk to the blender and blend in the lecithin, maple syrup, and vanilla. Store in an airtight container in the fridge for up to 5 days.

TIP: If you're using lecithin granules and find the creamer just doesn't want to blend smooth, pulse the granules first in a spice grinder.

TRY THIS: Turn this into a specialty creamer by adding ¼ teaspoon hazelnut extract.

Buttermilk

. . . .

MAKES ABOUT 2 CUPS

Do you keep scrolling past recipes for buttermilk pancakes and biscuits because they seem impossible to veganize? Well, now you have the secret to fluffy, light pancakes and classic, flaky, pull-apart biscuits (psst . . . it's vinegar).

INGREDIENTS

¼ cup raw cashews, soaked in water for 6 hours

2 cups unsweetened nondairy milk

2 tablespoons apple cider vinegar

INSTRUCTIONS

1. Drain and rinse the soaked cashews.
2. In a blender, combine all of the ingredients and blend until smooth. Let the mixture sit for 15 minutes before using. The buttermilk can also be stored in an airtight container in the fridge for 1 to 2 days.

Simple Sour Cream

· ·

MAKES 1¾ CUPS

This cream is a great substitute whenever you need sour cream. It's subtly sour, but you can always add more lemon juice or vinegar, if desired, or jazz it up by using the garlic variation at the bottom of the recipe. Like most creams in this book, this gets better after chilling.

INGREDIENTS

1½ cups raw cashews, soaked in water for 6 hours

2 tablespoons fresh lemon juice

2 teaspoons apple cider vinegar

½ teaspoon sea salt

TRY THIS: We sometimes add 1 small garlic clove and ½ teaspoon Dijon mustard to the blender to give this simple sour cream a little more oomph. This version makes a flavorful topping for tacos, burritos, or baked potatoes.

INSTRUCTIONS

1. Drain and rinse the soaked cashews.
2. In a blender, combine all the ingredients with ½ cup water and blend until very smooth. Test for smoothness by rubbing a bit of the mixture between your thumb and index finger—you should not feel any grittiness. Transfer to an airtight container and store in the fridge for up to 2 weeks. The cream will thicken once refrigerated.

Coconut Yogurt

MAKES ABOUT 1¼ CUPS

I had been experimenting (aka struggling) with almond and cashew versions of this recipe for a few days when my friend Gena (of Choosing Raw.com) posted a coconut milk yogurt recipe on her blog. It was so simple and had the smooth texture I had been chasing. I toasted her genius from my kitchen and went about creating a fermented version that would be perfectly thick and blissfully creamy. Ta-da! This coconut concoction is just as versatile as a traditional yogurt. It works beautifully in a bowl, topped with granola and fresh berries, and adds the ideal texture to a tzatziki sauce when blended with salt, garlic, and cucumber. —L. P.

Fermented foods contain Lactobacillus acidophilus, which is essential for gut health. Lactobacillus acidophilus has been shown to aid in digestion, and reduce gas and stomach upset, as well as improve the function of your immune system. Many cultures have been consuming fermented foods for centuries. Common fermented foods include yogurt, kefir, kombucha, kimchi, miso, pickles, and sauerkraut.

INGREDIENTS

1 (13.5-ounce) can full-fat coconut milk, chilled in the fridge for at least 8 hours

½ teaspoon probiotic powder

2 teaspoons agave nectar or pure maple syrup

2 teaspoons fresh lemon juice

Pinch of sea salt

INSTRUCTIONS

1. Scoop out the layer of solid coconut cream from the top of the can and transfer it to a small bowl. (You can save the liquid remaining at the bottom of the can for making smoothies or for thinning the yogurt as suggested in the Try This, below.)
2. Add the probiotic powder and stir to combine. Cover the bowl with a clean tea towel and set aside at room temperature to ferment. Depending on the level of tartness you desire, ferment the yogurt for 24 to 48 hours.
3. Add the agave nectar, lemon juice, and salt and stir to combine. Store in an airtight container in the fridge for up to 7 days.

TRY THIS: This yogurt has a thick, almost Greek yogurt—like texture. If you'd like a thinner yogurt, add up to ½ cup of the liquid from the coconut milk can prior to the fermentation process. The yogurt will thicken as it ferments and again when it chills. You can play with this ratio to get the perfect consistency for parfaits, frozen yogurt (see page xx), and dips.

Better Butter

Butter is something we can live without, but we can't deny others' love for it. What makes this butter better is that it contains plant-based fats and acts just like dairy-based butter: it's hard when it's cold, it's soft at room temperature, and it melts when spread on toast. The use of refined coconut oil gives it a mild flavor perfect for baking or cooking. Try replacing the conventional butter in your next batch of cookies, and you may never go back.

INGREDIENTS

½ cup melted refined coconut oil

¼ cup unsweetened nondairy milk

2 tablespoons olive oil

1 teaspoon sunflower lecithin liquid, or 2 teaspoons soy lecithin granules

1 teaspoon maca powder

¼ teaspoon fresh lemon juice

¼ teaspoon xanthan gum

Pinch of turmeric

Pinch of sea salt

INSTRUCTIONS

1. In a food processor (or a blender, if using lecithin granules), combine all the ingredients and process for 2 full minutes, or until the lecithin has fully dissolved and the mixture is smooth.

2. Pour into a small silicone mold or container and refrigerate until solidified, at least 2 hours. Store in the fridge in a covered container for up to 1 month.

Cream Cheese

. . . .

MAKES 1½ CUPS

Love a crisp, toasted bagel smothered in cream cheese? Let me introduce you to this incredible, dairy-free alternative to my favorite cheese spread. It's tangy, creamy, and a whole lotta dreamy. Add flair by mixing in your favorite fresh herbs like minced chives and parsley. —N. A.

INGREDIENTS

1½ cups raw cashews, soaked in water for 6 hours

½ teaspoon probiotic powder

2 tablespoons melted coconut oil

1 teaspoon fresh lemon juice

½ teaspoon cane sugar (optional)

½ teaspoon sea salt

INSTRUCTIONS

1. Drain and rinse the soaked cashews.
2. In a blender, combine the cashews, ¾ cup water, and the probiotic powder and blend on high speed until super smooth. Test for smoothness by rubbing a bit of the mixture between your thumb and index finger—you should not feel any grittiness.
3. Line a strainer with a few layers of cheesecloth or a nut milk bag and set it over a bowl. Pour the blended cashews into the cheesecloth. Pull up and twist the ends of the cheesecloth together so it is somewhat tight around the cashew mixture. Set aside to ferment for 24 hours. Pick a warm place, like inside your oven with the light on or on top of your refrigerator, to further promote fermentation.
4. Transfer the fermented cashew mixture to a food processor, add the coconut oil, lemon juice, cane sugar, and salt, and process until combined and smooth. Transfer the cream cheese to an airtight container and store in the fridge for up to 1 month. It will thicken once refrigerated.

Cashew Coffee Creamer (page 42)
and Cream Cheese (page 47)

Cultured Nut Cheese

· ·

MAKES ONE 8 X 12-INCH CHEESE LOG

If you've never cultured your own nut cheese, this is a great recipe to start with. You will be surprised that, by following a few simple steps, you'll soon be creating creamy, spreadable cheese at home. You'll see that this recipe, like those for most of our cheeses, calls for probiotic powder. There are quite a few vegan probiotic brands on the market. We like both Trophic and NuChapter, but you'll surely find your own favorite at your local health food store. You can buy probiotic capsules or just the powder; if you pick up capsules, just make sure they are gelatin-free (usually it says "vegan" right on the label). Now, find some counter space and soak those cashews.

INGREDIENTS

2 cups raw cashews, soaked in water for 6 hours

1 teaspoon probiotic powder

2 teaspoons nutritional yeast flakes

½ teaspoon sea salt

Finely chopped fresh herbs or spices of your choice, for rolling

INSTRUCTIONS

1. Drain and rinse the soaked cashews.
2. In a blender, combine the cashews, probiotic powder, and ½ cup water. Blend until completely smooth (be patient). If additional water is required, add up to 2 tablespoons more, a little at a time, to ensure that you're getting a perfectly smooth texture with as little water as possible. You will need to blend it for a couple of minutes to get the texture just right. Test for smoothness by rubbing a teaspoon of the mixture between your thumb and index finger. If the texture feels gritty, keep blending.
3. Pour the mixture into a strainer lined with cheesecloth or a nut milk bag. Place the strainer over a bowl and set aside to ferment for 24 to 36 hours. Pick a warm place, like inside your oven with the light on or on top of your refrigerator, to further promote fermentation. It is also helpful to set a jar or a can on top of the cheese to add just enough weight to press out any extra liquid, resulting in a thicker cheese.
4. Transfer the cheese to a bowl and stir in the nutritional yeast and salt.

TRY THIS: This recipe makes a smooth, spreadable cheese. To make a firmer version, see the air-drying technique in the Date and Fig Cashew Cheese recipe on page 58.

5. Turn out the cheese onto a piece of parchment paper and use the parchment to roll the cheese into a log shape. Fold in the ends of the parchment to cover the cheese and store the log in the refrigerator. It will firm up as it cools.
6. Before serving, roll the log of cheese in fresh herbs of your choice (tarragon, basil, or parsley) or spices such as black pepper, steak spice, or dukkah.

Easy Cheese

· ·

MAKES ABOUT 1¼ CUPS

Although our first bite of fermented vegan cheese completely revolutionized our culinary repertories, we live in the real world, with full-time jobs, to-do lists that seem to grow every day, and families who refuse to wait a week for a cheesy dinner. So, when we have time to prep ahead, we make the fancy fermented version, and when we don't, we make this one. Just soak those cashews when you get up, and you'll be serving an amazing entrée covered in slices of creamy, garlicky, cheesy goodness by six P.M.

INGREDIENTS

1 cup raw cashews, soaked in water for 6 hours

3 tablespoons fresh lemon juice

1 tablespoon nutritional yeast flakes

½ teaspoon sea salt

¼ teaspoon garlic powder

¼ teaspoon white miso

INSTRUCTIONS

1. Drain and rinse the soaked cashews.
2. In a food processor, combine all of the ingredients and process until smooth. Transfer to a container and refrigerate for at least 1 hour to firm up the cheese.
3. Once firm, spoon the cheese onto a rectangular piece of plastic wrap. Wrap the cheese tightly in the plastic wrap, twisting the ends to form a log shape. Store in the fridge for 5 to 7 days.

TIP: Slice the cheese over salads, spread on bread for sandwiches, or stir in chopped basil or thyme and pipe into shells to serve smothered in tomato sauce (see page 130).

Clockwise from bottom left: Date and Fig Cashew Cheese (page 58), Spicy Jalapeño Cheese (page 56), Cultured Nut Cheese (page 49), and Cheddar Cheese (page 52)

Cheddar Cheese

Cheese is usually the last thing to keep vegetarians from making the final switch to veganism. Cheddar, specifically, is the go-to for quesadillas, nachos, and grilled cheese sandwiches, and we'd be willing to bet there's a block in most people's refrigerators. Who can blame them? It's salty and tangy and full of fat, all things our bodies crave. This made-from-scratch cheddar has all the qualities of the dairy-based stuff but is made with plants and doesn't cause harm to animals or our bodies in the process. And it's a simple process at that—you'll be slicing, dicing, and grating before you know it.

INGREDIENTS

1 cup raw cashews, soaked in water for 6 hours

½ teaspoon probiotic powder

¼ cup agar flakes, or 2½ teaspoons agar powder

½ cup nutritional yeast flakes

1½ tablespoons mellow brown rice miso

½ teaspoon sea salt

¼ teaspoon xanthan gum

1 tablespoon coconut oil

Canola oil or other neutral oil, for the pan

INSTRUCTIONS

1. Drain and rinse the soaked cashews.
2. In a blender, combine the cashews, ½ cup water, and the probiotic powder and blend until completely smooth. This takes a little patience, but it will improve the texture of the cheese if you ensure there is no grittiness left. Test for smoothness by rubbing a bit of the mixture between your thumb and index finger. If it feels gritty, keep blending. Transfer the mixture to a glass or ceramic bowl, cover, and let sit at room temperature for 24 to 36 hours (the longer it sits, the sharper the flavor will be).
3. In a small saucepan, whisk together ¾ cup water and the agar. Bring to a boil over medium heat, then reduce the heat to low and simmer for 10 minutes, whisking often to ensure that the flakes don't stick to the bottom of the pan.
4. While the liquid is cooking, combine the fermented cashew mixture, nutritional yeast, miso, salt, and xanthan gum in a food processor. Process for about 2 minutes, until very smooth.
5. When the agar mixture has finished cooking, remove from the heat and whisk in the coconut oil. Add this mixture to the cashew mixture in

the food processor and process to combine. A very smooth, shiny texture should develop.

6. Lightly oil a mini loaf pan (6 x 3 inches) or other pan of equivalent size. Quickly scoop the mixture into the pan and use a spatula to smooth out the top. Allow to cool at room temperature for about 1 hour. Refrigerate until firm, at least 2 hours. Remove from pan (it should just slide right out) and serve. Store any leftovers tightly wrapped in plastic wrap in the fridge for up to 1 month.

Buffalo Mozzarella

· ·

Missing that summer salad staple, composed of stacks of sliced tomato, creamy mozzarella, and bright, bold basil leaves? The wait is over—vegan mozzarella is here. This recipe makes what seemed impossible undeniably easy. Sure, it takes some time to prepare, but think of it as a B plot: a few minutes of effort here and there in between your life's A-plot adventures (work, sleep, play). When it's time for the exciting culmination, your mozzarella will be ready to star in a Caprese salad, amid roasted vegetables or thinly sliced atop a classic Neapolitan pizza.

INGREDIENTS

1 cup raw cashews, soaked in water for 6 hours

½ teaspoon probiotic powder

2 teaspoons nutritional yeast flakes

1 teaspoon xanthan gum

½ teaspoon sea salt

¼ cup agar flakes, or 2¼ teaspoons agar powder

> **TIP:** We suggest using a serrated knife to slice the mozzarella; it makes lovely thin slices without mashing the beautiful ball of mozzarella.

INSTRUCTIONS

1. Drain and rinse the soaked cashews.
2. In a blender, combine the cashews, probiotic powder, and ½ cup water and blend until smooth. Pour into a glass or ceramic bowl, cover with a clean tea towel, and set aside to ferment for 24 hours.
3. In a blender, combine the fermented cashew mixture, nutritional yeast, xanthan gum, and salt and blend until smooth and creamy.
4. In a small saucepan, whisk together the agar and ⅔ cup water. Bring to a boil over medium heat, then reduce the heat to low and simmer, whisking often, for 10 minutes until all the agar has dissolved and the liquid begins to thicken.
5. In a shallow medium bowl, combine the blended cashew mixture and the agar mixture. Whisk until the agar mixture is completely incorporated.
6. Transfer the bowl to the fridge to chill for 15 minutes.
7. Divide the cheese into quarters. Put each portion on a square piece of plastic wrap. Pull the corners of the plastic wrap together over the cheese and twist to form the cheese into a tight ball, just like the classic buffalo mozzarella shape. Return to the fridge to chill for an additional hour or two before slicing. Store any leftovers tightly wrapped in plastic wrap in the fridge for up to 1 week.

Spicy Jalapeño Cheese

· ·

MAKES ONE 4-INCH WHEEL

Add a little heat to your next nondairy cheese plate with this spicy and tangy wheel. Much like other cheeses in this book, this one requires a little extra time since it needs to be air-dried for about a week (but the actual hands-on time is minimal). You'll be awarded with a sliceable, aged cheese that pairs so well with crackers and wine that you'll want to have parties every week just for an excuse to make it again.

INGREDIENTS

1½ cups raw cashews, soaked in water for 6 hours

½ teaspoon probiotic powder

1½ tablespoons nutritional yeast flakes

2 teaspoons mellow white miso

2 teaspoons seeded and minced jalapeño

½ teaspoon red pepper flakes

½ teaspoon sea salt, plus more for coating

INSTRUCTIONS

1. Drain and rinse the soaked cashews.
2. In a blender, combine the cashews, probiotic powder, and ¾ cup water and blend until completely smooth. This takes a little patience, but it will improve the texture of the cheese if you ensure that there is no grittiness left. Test for smoothness by rubbing a bit of the mixture between your thumb and index finger. If it feels gritty, keep blending.
3. Line a sieve with a few layers of cheesecloth or a nut milk bag and set it over a bowl. Pour the blended cashews into the cheesecloth. Pull up and twist the ends of the cheesecloth together so it is somewhat tight around the cashew mixture. Set a jar or can on top for a little weight. Set aside to ferment for 36 hours at room temperature.
4. Transfer the cheese mixture to a small bowl (discard the liquid that was pressed out of the cheese as it fermented) and stir in the nutritional yeast, miso, jalapeño, red pepper flakes, and salt.
5. Press the cheese into a 4-inch ring mold or mini springform cake pan. Firm in the freezer for 1 hour, or until solidified.
6. Remove from the freezer and gently press the cheese out of the ring. Wet your hands, coat them in salt, and gently rub the salt over the

entire surface of the cheese. Set the cheese on a piece of parchment paper on top of a cooling rack and allow to air-dry at room temperature for about 3 days. Use the parchment paper to flip the cheese over directly onto the rack (discard the parchment) and allow to air-dry for 3 to 4 days more, or until it develops a rind and becomes firm enough to slice. The cheese will keep in the fridge, wrapped tightly in plastic wrap, for 2 to 3 months.

Date and Fig Cashew Cheese

· ·

MAKES ONE 4-INCH WHEEL

Round out your cheese plate with this sweet addition, a smattering of Pecan and Raisin Rice Crackers (page 96), and, of course, juicy red grapes. The caramel-like flavor of the dates along with the figs' wine undertones beautifully balance the tanginess of this air-aged artisan cheese. On the sweeter side, it is ideal as an appetizer or a dessert course.

INGREDIENTS

1 cup raw cashews, soaked in water for 6 hours

½ teaspoon probiotic powder

1 Medjool date, pitted and finely chopped

1 dried fig, finely chopped

1 tablespoon nutritional yeast flakes

1 teaspoon fresh lemon juice

½ teaspoon white miso

¼ teaspoon sea salt, plus more for coating

TIP: Fermenting and air-aging impact the sourness of your cheese. Once you're comfortable with the technique, adjust the time period for your preferred level of tang. The air-aging technique also works with the basic fermented cashew cheese recipe to make it firm and sliceable. Give it a try on page 50.

INSTRUCTIONS

1. Drain and rinse the soaked cashews.
2. In a blender, combine the cashews, probiotic powder, and ½ cup water and blend until completely smooth. Test for smoothness by rubbing a teaspoon of the mixture between your thumb and index finger. If the texture feels gritty, keep blending. This takes a little patience, but it will improve the texture of the cheese if you ensure that there is no grittiness left.
3. Transfer the mixture to a fine-mesh metal sieve lined with cheesecloth or a nut milk bag. Set the sieve over a bowl and set a jar or can on top of the cheese mixture for a little weight. Set aside to ferment for 36 hours at room temperature.
4. Transfer the cheese mixture to a small bowl (discard the liquid that was pressed out of the cheese as it fermented) and stir in the date, fig, yeast, lemon juice, miso, and salt. Press the cheese into a ring mold or a mini springform cake pan. Firm in the freezer for 1 hour.
5. Remove from the freezer and gently press the cheese out of the ring. Coat your hands in salt and gently rub the salt over the surface of the cheese. Set the cheese on a cooling rack and allow to air-dry for 4 days. Store in the fridge, wrapped tightly in plastic wrap, for 2 to 3 months.

Classic Cheese Ball (page 60) and
Super-Seedy Crackers (page 97)

Classic Cheese Ball

· ·

MAKES ONE ½-CUP BALL

If you're ready to take your cheese-making mastery to the masses, here is an impressive cheese ball centerpiece you can present at your next party. The cheese ball can be made well in advance, but it will soften at room temperature, so keep it in the freezer until a little before the party starts, then roll it in all the goodies and set it in the center of your table with some beautiful seedy crackers (see page 97) to impress your guests. This was a favorite among our testers, who tried to convince us it made only a single serving.

INGREDIENTS

½ cup Cultured Nut Cheese (page 49)

1 clove garlic, grated

1 teaspoon apple cider vinegar

1 tablespoon finely sliced scallion (green and white parts) or chives

2 tablespoons Coconut Bacon Bits (page 101), crumbled

1 tablespoon finely chopped pecans

Crackers, raw vegetables, and bread, for serving

INSTRUCTIONS

1. In a small bowl, stir together the cheese, garlic, and vinegar.
2. Line a small bowl with plastic wrap and fill it with the cheese mixture. This will mold the cheese into a round shape. Chill in the freezer for 20 minutes to firm the cheese.
3. In a medium bowl, stir together the scallion, bacon, and pecans.
4. Remove the cheese from the freezer and lift it from the bowl using the plastic wrap; remove and discard the plastic wrap. Roll the ball of cheese in the bowl of coating ingredients until well coated. Serve with crackers, raw vegetables, and bread.

> **TIP:** Crumbling and finely chopping the garnishes into small pieces makes it easier for them to adhere to the cheese ball and distributes the flavors evenly in each bite when you spread the cheese over a cracker.

Fruity Soft Serve

· ·

SERVES 2

We believe we've told everyone we know about the great banana transformation. But just in case you've been out of earshot, trust us, you must make this. And you must be patient and believe. When you put those bananas in your food processor and they jump around and become chunky, you will doubt. We all doubted. But scrape down the sides and keep believing, and you will be rewarded with the most incredible, fruit-based soft serve you could ever imagine. Even though we've made it at least a thousand times, we are still impressed. It is the perfect summer treat, the best breakfast going, and a super-satisfying post-workout, potassium-packed snack.

INGREDIENTS

2 ripe bananas, peeled, cut into quarters, and frozen

1 cup chopped fruit (mango, raspberry, strawberry, blueberry, peach, etc.; optional)

TRY THIS: You can also jazz this up by pulsing in a tablespoon or two of chocolate chips, nut butter, or coconut butter at the end. To serve this treat, we like to set up a soft-serve bar with lots of fun toppings (chopped nuts, dried fruit, coconut, granola, etc.) as an awesome brunch for a family with lots of little ones. They love the idea of having ice cream for breakfast and don't care at all that it is completely made of fruit.

INSTRUCTIONS

1. In a food processor, process the bananas until they become soft and creamy—exactly like soft serve. The bananas will first break down into small chunks, but keep going and be patient. Scrape down the sides, if needed, and continue to process until the bananas are completely broken down and become thick, smooth, and glossy.
2. If you're adding fruit, this is the time to pour it in. Process until well incorporated; leave a few chunks of fruit if that's your preference or process into a smooth, soft-serve texture. Serve immediately.

Vanilla Bean Ice Cream

• •

MAKES ABOUT 4 CUPS

I remember my grandparents always had vanilla ice cream on hand, and my sister and I would follow their lead and load it up with chocolate fudge, caramel sauce, peanuts, and fruit. It was the perfect end to every meal we shared with them. This particular recipe is delicious on its own, but I've included a few fun flavor variations, too, because, well, I'd like to think I learned from the best ice cream eaters in town. You can also use it to make Ice Cream Cone Confections (page 230) or Ice Cream Sandwiches (page 229). —N. A.

INGREDIENTS

1 (13.5-ounce) can full-fat coconut milk

1 cup unsweetened nondairy milk

½ cup pure maple syrup

¼ cup cane sugar

3 tablespoons melted coconut oil

½ teaspoon vanilla bean powder, or 2 vanilla beans, halved lengthwise and seeds scraped

½ teaspoon xanthan gum

INSTRUCTIONS

1. In a blender, combine the coconut milk, nondairy milk, maple syrup, cane sugar, coconut oil, and vanilla and blend until smooth. Add the xanthan gum and blend briefly on low speed to incorporate.

2. Transfer the mixture to a shallow bowl and refrigerate until thoroughly chilled, about 3 hours.

3. Transfer the chilled ice cream base to your ice cream maker and churn according to the manufacturer's instructions. If you're after a soft-serve treat, serve as soon as the process is finished. Otherwise, transfer the ice cream to an airtight container and place a piece of parchment paper on the surface, pressing down lightly (this prevents ice crystals from forming on the surface) before sealing with the lid. Store in the freezer. For best texture, consume within 2 weeks.

TRY THESE FLAVOR VARIATIONS: *Chocolate Swirl:* Once the ice cream has been churned, scoop one-third of the ice cream into a container. Drizzle Simple Chocolate Syrup (page 195) on top. Cover with another third of the ice cream and add another drizzle of syrup. Repeat until all the ice cream has been used, then top with one last drizzle of syrup.

Cookie Dough: Add chunks of unbaked Cookie Dough (page 220) at the end of the churning process.

Strawberry Cheesecake: Once the ice cream has been churned, scoop one-third of the ice cream into a container. Scatter teaspoons of Strawberry Chia Jam (page 111) and crushed Cinnamon Graham Crackers (page 225) on top. Cover with another third of the ice cream, then another layer of jam and graham crackers. Top with the remaining ice cream.

Chocolate Ice Cream

MAKES ABOUT 4 CUPS

This creamy, intensely chocolate ice cream will remind you of your favorite double scoop. Serve it as is or jazz it up with a drizzle of Quick Caramel Sauce (page 194) or Simple Chocolate Syrup (page 195) and a handful of berries or toasted nuts.

INGREDIENTS

1 (13.5-ounce) can full-fat coconut milk

1 cup unsweetened nondairy milk

⅔ cup cocoa powder

½ cup pure maple syrup

¼ cup coconut sugar

¼ cup strong coffee, chilled

1 teaspoon pure vanilla extract

Pinch of sea salt

½ teaspoon xanthan gum

INSTRUCTIONS

1. In a blender, combine the coconut milk, nondairy milk, cocoa powder, maple syrup, coconut sugar, coffee, vanilla, and salt and blend until smooth. Add the xanthan gum and blend briefly on low speed to incorporate.
2. Transfer the mixture to a shallow bowl and refrigerate until thoroughly chilled, about 3 hours.
3. Transfer the chilled ice cream base to an ice cream maker and churn according to the manufacturer's instructions. If you're after a soft-serve treat, serve as soon as the process is finished. Otherwise, transfer the ice cream to an airtight container and place a piece of parchment paper on the surface, pressing down lightly (this prevents ice crystals from forming on the surface) before sealing with the lid. Store in the freezer. For best texture, consume within 2 weeks.

Frozen Yogurt

. . . .

MAKES ABOUT 3¼ CUPS

Do you remember those little frozen yogurt carts with the blocks of plain frozen yogurt wrapped in paper, and the containers of frozen raspberries, strawberries, peaches, and mango? You'd watch the alchemy as a white block of yogurt went into the chute, followed by a cup of frozen fruit, then with one little pull of that metal slot-machine handle, you'd have a pink, purple, or peach spiral sitting atop your cone. It was magnificent. Now you can create the same magic in your own home. You won't even need a wand to replace the excitement of the slot-machine payout moment—one bite of a strawberry coconut cone, and you'll believe you've hit the jackpot.

INGREDIENTS

2 (13.5-ounce) cans full-fat coconut milk, chilled in the fridge for at least 8 hours

1 teaspoon probiotic powder

⅓ cup plus 2 teaspoons agave nectar or pure maple syrup

1 tablespoon plus 2 teaspoons fresh lemon juice

½ teaspoon pure vanilla extract

Generous pinch of sea salt

TRY THIS: Add your favorite fruit at the blending stage of the recipe to make a wonderful frozen concoction. Strawberries, raspberries, and blueberries are personal favorites, but try cherries, blackberries, peaches, or mango if you're feeling adventurous. We like to add 2 cups chopped fruit to the frozen yogurt recipe.

INSTRUCTIONS

1. Scoop out the solid coconut cream from one of the cans of coconut milk and transfer it to a medium bowl (save the remaining liquid to add to smoothies). Add the entire contents of the second can to the bowl.
2. Add the probiotic powder to the bowl and stir until well incorporated. Cover the bowl with a clean tea towel and set aside at room temperature to ferment for 48 hours.
3. Pour the coconut yogurt into a blender and add the agave nectar, lemon juice, vanilla, and salt. Blend to combine.
4. Chill for 1 hour in the fridge.
5. Transfer the chilled frozen yogurt base to an ice cream maker and churn according to the manufacturer's instructions (typically 20 to 25 minutes). Serve immediately or transfer to an airtight container and freeze until hardened to the desired consistency. Store in the freezer for 4 to 6 weeks.

From top left: Go-Anywhere Chia Cereal (page 76),
Good Morning Muesli (page 75), Basic Nut/Seed Milk
(page 37), Chocolate Buckwheat Crunch (page 69), and
Cinnamon Toast Cereal (page 73).

CHAPTER 4

Better-Than-Store-Bought Cereals and Snacks

· ·

THERE IS NOTHING BETTER THAN waking up to a big breakfast made exactly the way you like it (or falling asleep dreaming about it). In this chapter, we're going to show you how to re-create your favorite breakfast recipes at home to ensure a fresh, delicious start to every day. And staying fueled with hearty, healthful snacks that rival all of your packaged favorites means staving off that afternoon slump.

These reliable recipes can be made ahead (we know everyone could use a few extra minutes to get out the door or hit the snooze button) and even enjoyed on the go. The cereals, breakfast bars, and oatmeal sold in stores and coffee shops contain countless additives and fillers; get rid of all those extras by preparing these convenient essentials at home in minutes.

Maple Date Granola

MAKES 5 CUPS

I am such a cereal girl. Truth be told, I used to eat it dry, by the handful, when I was too lazy to make a proper meal. Ironically, it was one of the first convenience foods I ditched from my pantry many years ago. In its place came homemade granola, one of the easiest and most versatile cereals you can create yourself. This crunchy, maple-and-date-sweetened version has become a staple. It also makes the house smell amazing, like you've been slaving in the kitchen all day. —N. A.

INGREDIENTS

2 cups rolled oats

½ cup raw buckwheat groats (not kasha)

¼ cup raw sunflower seeds

1 teaspoon ground cinnamon

¼ teaspoon sea salt

½ cup pure maple syrup

¾ cup pitted Medjool or honey dates

2 tablespoons melted coconut oil

1 tablespoon flax meal

1 teaspoon pure vanilla extract

INSTRUCTIONS

1. Preheat the oven to 300°F. Line a baking sheet with parchment paper.
2. In a large bowl, combine the oats, buckwheat groats, sunflower seeds, cinnamon, and salt.
3. In a blender, combine the maple syrup, ¼ cup of the dates, the coconut oil, flax meal, vanilla, and 2 tablespoons water and blend on high speed until smooth. Pour the liquid mixture into the bowl with the dry ingredients and stir to coat.
4. Spread the granola evenly over the prepared baking sheet and bake for 30 minutes, rotating the pan and stirring gently halfway through (if you overstir, the granola won't stick together as well).
5. While the granola is baking, chop the remaining ½ cup dates.
6. Remove the granola from the oven and sprinkle the chopped dates over the top. Let cool, untouched, for at least 20 minutes. The granola will harden as it cools. Store in an airtight container at room temperature for up to 3 weeks, or in the freezer for up to 5 months.

Chocolate Buckwheat Crunch

MAKES ABOUT 5 CUPS

Buckwheat is often touted for what it doesn't have, namely gluten (yes, even though it has the word *wheat* in its name). But we love it for what it does have: a great crunchy texture and incredible binding ability. Buckwheat is generally used like a grain but is actually a fruit seed. And, like most seeds, it is packed with goodness: tons of protein, fiber, amino acids, and minerals. So, with buckwheat as its base, this is a true cereal standout. Enjoy this chocolaty, crunchy powerhouse in a bowl with Easy Almond Milk (page 38) or paired with Coconut Yogurt (page 45), or simply by the handful straight from the jar.

INGREDIENTS

2 cups raw buckwheat groats (not kasha)

1 cup chopped walnuts

1 cup raw sunflower seeds

½ cup large coconut flakes

2 tablespoons chia meal

Pinch of sea salt

8 Medjool dates, pitted and chopped

¼ cup pure maple syrup

¼ cup coconut oil

¼ cup cocoa powder

2 tablespoons coconut sugar

2 tablespoons unsweetened almond milk

½ teaspoon pure vanilla extract

2 tablespoons hemp hearts

INSTRUCTIONS

1. Preheat the oven to 350°F. Line a baking sheet with parchment paper.
2. In a large bowl, stir together the buckwheat groats, walnuts, sunflower seeds, coconut flakes, chia meal, salt, and dates.
3. In a small saucepan, combine the maple syrup, coconut oil, cocoa powder, coconut sugar, almond milk, and vanilla and whisk together over medium heat. Whisk until the cocoa powder is completely incorporated and the coconut oil has melted, 1 to 2 minutes.
4. Pour the wet mixture over the dry mixture and stir until well coated.
5. Transfer the buckwheat mixture to the prepared baking sheet. Spread it into an even layer.
6. Bake for 25 minutes, stirring at least twice during the baking time to make sure the bits on the edges don't burn. Remove from the oven and sprinkle with the hemp hearts. Let cool completely, then break into chunks and transfer to an airtight container. Store in the fridge or pantry for 4 to 6 weeks.

TRY THIS: This is a great snack to have around. Feel free to play with other additions or variations, swap in other nuts like cashews to replace the walnuts, or up the exotic flavors by adding some chopped crystallized ginger or goji berries.

Vanilla Almond Granola (opposite)
and Coconut Yogurt (page 45)

Vanilla Almond Granola

. . . .

MAKES 6 CUPS

Cereal is a classic comfort food. When life is swirling around you, find a quiet space, pour a bowl of this crunchy, sweet, and fragrant granola, and spoon slowly. Soon your world will be all vanilla infused and you'll have the energy to tackle another e-mail, answer another question, and navigate what's next on your to-do list. And if even that slow moment is too much time to set aside, this granola packs perfectly for a portable snack to savor.

INGREDIENTS

2 cups rolled oats

1 cup chopped raw almonds

¾ cup large coconut flakes

¼ cup Medjool dates, pitted and chopped

2 tablespoons uncooked quinoa

1 vanilla bean, halved lengthwise and seeds scraped

1 teaspoon sea salt

1 cup unsweetened applesauce

½ cup pure maple syrup

4 teaspoons pure vanilla extract

2 tablespoons coconut oil, melted

INSTRUCTIONS

1. Preheat the oven to 300°F. Line two baking sheets with parchment paper.
2. In a medium bowl, mix together the oats, almonds, coconut, dates, quinoa, vanilla bean seeds, and salt.
3. In another bowl, stir together the applesauce, maple syrup, vanilla extract, and coconut oil until smooth.
4. Pour the wet ingredients over the dry ingredients and stir until well combined.
5. Spread the granola evenly over the prepared baking sheets and bake for 55 to 60 minutes, stirring every 15 minutes. Halfway through baking, rotate the pans and swap them between the racks in your oven (top to bottom, bottom to top) to be sure the granola bakes evenly. Let cool completely on the baking sheets. Store in an airtight container at room temperature for up to 3 weeks, or in the freezer for up to 5 months.

TIP: Even though you can fit all the granola on one tray, don't do it. The granola needs space so it can crisp up in the oven. When it is all touching, it just steams and remains soft and wet. Divide the mixture between two baking sheets.

Clockwise from top left: Cinnamon Toast Cereal (opposite), Good Morning Muesli (page 75), Chocolate Buckwheat Crunch (page 69), and Go-Anywhere Chia Cereal (page 76)

Cinnamon Toast Cereal

MAKES 5 CUPS

Fold down the corner of this page. If you love cinnamon-flavored cereal as much as we do, you're going to want to come back to this recipe a lot. Think of it as a template for your perfect breakfast bowl. Bake the cereal while you make yourself a cup of coffee or squeeze some fresh juice, pour the cereal into a large bowl, and add whatever toppings you have on hand—a sprinkle of hemp hearts and a few slices of banana, or goji berries and pecans and a splash of almond milk—and take pleasure in the fact that you can make cereal that's better than the boxed stuff.

INGREDIENTS

3 cups puffed brown rice cereal

2 cups puffed quinoa

4 teaspoons ground cinnamon

1 teaspoon ground ginger

½ teaspoon sea salt

3 tablespoons pure maple syrup

2 tablespoons melted coconut oil

Optional add-ins: sunflower seeds, hemp hearts, pumpkin seeds, nuts, dried fruit

INSTRUCTIONS

1. Preheat the oven to 350°F. Line a large rimmed baking pan with parchment paper.
2. In a large bowl, combine the puffed brown rice, puffed quinoa, cinnamon, ginger, and salt. Add the maple syrup and coconut oil and stir until all the cereal is coated.
3. Spread the cereal evenly over the prepared pan and bake for 12 to 15 minutes, until dry to the touch, stirring halfway through. Let cool completely. Mix in the optional add-ins, if desired. Store in an airtight container at room temperature for about 1 month.

Creamy Five-Grain Porridge

· ·

MAKES 8 SERVINGS

This creamy hot cereal is made from a blend of whole grains and takes less than five minutes to cook. It is perfect for busy mornings when you need to get your energy level up and keep it going all morning long. You can dress up this cereal with a handful of fresh or dried fruit, maple syrup, banana slices, or nut butter—whatever toppings you like.

INGREDIENTS

CEREAL MIX

½ cup uncooked short-grain brown rice

½ cup raw buckwheat groats (not kasha)

½ cup steel-cut oats

½ cup uncooked millet or amaranth

¼ cup organic cornmeal

½ teaspoon ground cinnamon

OPTIONAL ADD-INS FOR SERVING

Maple syrup or other sweetener, almond milk, raisins

TIP: Feel free to play with the proportions of grains based on your preference. Not a fan of buckwheat? Replace it with more oats! Love cinnamon? Double it! The important part is blending all the grains into a flour so they cook up nice and quick.

INSTRUCTIONS

1. To make the cereal mix: In a blender, combine all the ingredients and pulse until the mixture has the consistency of coarse flour. The cereal mix will keep in an airtight container at room temperature for up to 6 months.

2. To prepare porridge: For each serving, combine ¼ cup cereal mix with ¾ cup water in a small saucepan. Bring to a boil over medium-high heat. Reduce to maintain a simmer and cook, stirring continuously, for 3 to 5 minutes, or until thick and creamy. Serve immediately with maple syrup, almond milk, and raisins, if desired.

Good Morning Muesli

A big jar of this made-ahead muesli makes a great hostess gift for when you arrive for a weekend stay. Bring along a batch of Coconut Yogurt (page 45) and a pint of fresh berries, and they may never let you leave. Plus, it ensures that no matter where you're staying, you'll have something suitable and satisfying to start your day.

INGREDIENTS

MUESLI MIX

3 cups old-fashioned rolled oats

¼ cup chopped almonds

3 tablespoons sliced dried apricots

2 tablespoons flax meal

2 tablespoons chia seeds

2 tablespoons raw pumpkin seeds

2 tablespoons chopped pitted Medjool dates

1 teaspoon pumpkin pie spice, homemade (page 170) or store-bought

Pinch of sea salt

FOR SERVING

½ cup unsweetened nondairy milk

INSTRUCTIONS

1. To make the muesli mix: In a large bowl, stir together all the ingredients. The muesli mix will keep in an airtight container at room temperature for up to 1 month.
2. To prepare a serving: The night before serving, portion out approximately ¾ cup muesli mix into an airtight container and add the nondairy milk. Soak overnight in the fridge.

> **TIP:** If you don't have apricots, you can easily substitute other dry fruit, such as raisins, cranberries, or currants.

Go-Anywhere Chia Cereal

MAKES 8 SERVINGS

When people ask us how we possibly fit so much homemade goodness into our everyday routines, we share this little secret for morning magic. It takes minutes to mix up a big batch of this cereal ahead of time, and it basically makes itself every morning while we take our showers. Of course, you can make it extra special by adding fresh fruit, but even the basic blend offers plenty of protein and healthy fat to power us through a busy day.

INGREDIENTS

CHIA CEREAL MIX

1 cup chia seeds

¼ cup raw hemp hearts

¼ cup raw buckwheat groats (not kasha)

¼ cup cacao nibs

¼ cup dried goji berries, cranberries, cherries, or mulberries

¼ cup raisins

Pinch of sea salt

FOR SERVING

½ cup vanilla nondairy milk

Sliced fresh fruit (optional)

INSTRUCTIONS

1. To make the chia cereal mix: In a large bowl, combine all the ingredients. The chia cereal mix will keep in an airtight container at room temperature for up to 3 months.
2. To prepare a serving: Combine 3 tablespoons of the chia cereal mix with the nondairy milk and refrigerate for 20 minutes to overnight. Add sliced fruit to make it extra fancy.

Sunday Morning Overnight Oats Sundae

. . . .

MAKES 2 SERVINGS

I believe this recipe makes people fall in love. How? I'm glad you asked. Just imagine: you get to sleep in (because breakfast is already made), laze in bed with that lucky someone, or take the time to laugh with your little ones as you wake them up, or slip into a bath instead of a shower to give yourself some well-deserved relaxation time (you did prep breakfast!). And then, after just a couple of minutes of parfait building, you get to scoop out spoonfuls of a beautiful layered breakfast with all the flavors reminiscent of a sundae or banana split. Sounds like the perfect conditions to cultivate love. —L. P.

INGREDIENTS

1½ cups almond milk

⅔ cup rolled oats

¼ cup chia seeds

2 tablespoons almond or peanut butter

1 ripe banana, peeled and mashed

4 teaspoons pure maple syrup

1 teaspoon pure vanilla extract

2 tablespoons chocolate chips or finely chopped dark chocolate

2 tablespoons coarsely chopped walnuts

½ cup fresh berries

INSTRUCTIONS

1. In a medium bowl, combine the almond milk, oats, chia seeds, nut butter, banana, maple syrup, and vanilla. Stir until well combined. Cover and refrigerate overnight.
2. The next morning, divide a quarter of the oat mixture between two tall glasses or mason jars. Next, sprinkle ½ tablespoon each of the chocolate chips and the walnuts into each glass, followed by 2 tablespoons of the berries.
3. Repeat step 2 to create three more layers of each ingredient in each glass or jar. Serve immediately.

> **TIP:** Don't forget to really mash that banana—it should be easily incorporated into the liquid mixture. Also, if you want an extra five minutes of sleep time, you don't really need to layer the parfaits. Just add the toppings to your prepped jar and scoop away.

Cinnamon-Raisin Oats-to-Go

MAKES THREE ½-CUP SERVINGS

If you find yourself picking up those packets of instant oatmeal, then this simple recipe is your answer to saving time and money. You can prep ahead of time for a week of good morning eats. Don't let the cinnamon-walnut combination constrain you. Change it up with variations like dried cherries, shredded coconut, and a sprinkle of cardamom, or dried blueberries, cashews, and some Demerara sugar.

INGREDIENTS

INSTANT OATS MIX

1 cup rolled oats

⅓ cup raisins

2 tablespoons maple sugar or cane sugar

2 tablespoons chopped walnuts

1½ teaspoons ground cinnamon

½ teaspoon sea salt

INSTRUCTIONS

1. To make the instant oats mix: In a food processor, pulse the rolled oats for about 15 seconds. Combine the oats and the remaining ingredients in a small bowl. The instant oats mix will keep in an airtight container (or divided evenly into sandwich bags for on-the-go ease) at room temperature for 2 to 3 months.

2. To prepare instant oats: Pour ½ cup boiling water over ½ cup instant oats mix. Stir once. Cover and let stand for 5 minutes. Stir thoroughly and enjoy.

Ultimate Gluten-Free Bread

If you're unhappy with the dense, beany-flavored gluten-free bread you find at the store, give this recipe a go. Mixing the dough in a stand mixer or using a hand mixer is important because it creates air pockets and gives the dough a lighter texture. It makes great sandwiches and toast.

INGREDIENTS

1 cup gluten-free oat flour

½ cup millet flour

½ cup tapioca flour

½ cup potato starch
(not potato flour)

2 teaspoons fast-rising
dry yeast

2 teaspoons xanthan gum

1 teaspoon baking powder

½ teaspoon baking soda

½ teaspoon sea salt

3 tablespoons olive oil,
plus more for the pan

2 tablespoons pure
maple syrup

2 tablespoons chia or flax meal

2 teaspoons apple cider vinegar

TRY THIS: Add some cinnamon and raisins to create a nice breakfast bread, or even sun-dried tomatoes and herbs for a savory lunchtime loaf.

INSTRUCTIONS

1. Lightly oil a 9 x 5-inch loaf pan.
2. In the bowl of a stand mixer fitted with the whisk attachment, or in a large bowl using a hand mixer, whisk together the oat flour, millet flour, tapioca flour, potato starch, yeast, xanthan gum, baking powder, baking soda, and salt.
3. In a small saucepan, combine the olive oil, maple syrup, chia meal, vinegar, and 1¼ cups water. Cook over medium heat, whisking occasionally, for about 3 minutes, until warmed through. Remove from the heat and check the temperature with a cooking thermometer. You want the liquid to be between 120° and 130°F.
4. Add the liquid to the bowl with the flour mixture and mix on medium speed until a dough comes together. Continue mixing for a full 2 minutes, stopping to scrape down the sides of the bowl, if necessary. The dough will look like a thick muffin batter.
5. Scoop the dough into the prepared loaf pan and smooth out the top with a spatula. Cover with a clean kitchen towel and set the pan in a warm, draft-free place to rise for 20 to 30 minutes.
6. Preheat the oven to 350°F.
7. Bake for 45 minutes. Let cool briefly, then transfer to a cooling rack to cool completely before slicing, at least 1 hour. The bread can be stored tightly wrapped in plastic wrap in a zip-top or paper bag at room temperature for about 5 days. Or slice, wrap tightly in plastic wrap and then aluminum foil, and freeze for up to 1 month.

Whole-Grain and Seed Bread

. . . .

MAKES 1 LOAF

Being able to make your own bread feels very empowering, but our goal was to create a wholesome recipe that isn't a full-day process. The result: a bread that is substantially tastier than store-bought bread, isn't laden with preservatives, and is actually easier than you might think. Let this be your opportunity to get in the habit of baking bread from scratch. You'll be so happy you did (and you can thank us later).

INGREDIENTS

1½ cups spelt flour

1 cup unbleached all-purpose flour

½ cup rolled oats

2 tablespoons sunflower seeds

2 tablespoons uncooked quinoa

2 tablespoons sesame seeds

2 tablespoons flaxseeds

2 teaspoons fast-rising dry yeast

½ teaspoon sea salt

3 tablespoons olive oil, plus more for greasing

2 tablespoons pure maple syrup

INSTRUCTIONS

1. Oil a 9 x 5-inch loaf pan.
2. In the bowl of a stand mixer fitted with the dough hook, or in a large bowl using a wooden spoon, mix together the spelt flour, all-purpose flour, rolled oats, sunflower seeds, quinoa, sesame seeds, flaxseeds, yeast, and salt.
3. In a small saucepan, combine the olive oil, maple syrup, and 1¼ cups water. Cook over medium heat, whisking occasionally, for about 3 minutes, until warmed through. Remove from the heat and check the temperature with a cooking thermometer. You want the liquid to be between 120° and 130°F.
4. Add the liquid to the bowl with the flour mixture and mix on medium speed until a dough comes together (alternatively, mix by hand with a wooden spoon). Continue to mix for a full 2 minutes, stopping to scrape down the sides of the bowl, if necessary. Unlike traditional bread dough, this dough will be soft and sticky—just go with it.
5. Transfer the dough to a lightly oiled bowl, cover with a clean kitchen towel, and set in a warm, draft-free place to rise for 30 minutes.

Whole-Grain and Seed Bread (opposite),
Strawberry Chia Jam (page 111), and Better
Butter (page 46)

MAKE IT GLUTEN-FREE:
Try the Ultimate Gluten-Free Bread on page 79.

6. Preheat the oven to 350°F.

7. Punch down the dough and transfer it to the prepared loaf pan. Press down and smooth out the top with a spatula or the back of a spoon. Bake for 45 minutes. Let sit briefly, then transfer to a wire rack to cool completely before slicing. The bread can be stored tightly wrapped in plastic wrap or in a zip-top bag at room temperature for about 5 days. Or slice, wrap tightly in plastic wrap and then aluminum foil, and freeze for up to 1 month.

Quick Rise and Shine Cinnamon Rolls

· ·

MAKES 8 ROLLS

We love this recipe because it takes far less time than any traditional yeast-based cinnamon roll recipe and is more pleasing than the rolls that come in a tube. It makes use of a quick bread–style dough that gives a more cakelike texture but can have you enjoying fresh-out-of-the-oven cinnamon rolls in less than an hour. Just mix, roll, and bake!

INGREDIENTS

ROLLS

1½ cups nondairy milk, at room temperature, plus 1 table-spoon, for brushing

2 teaspoons apple cider vinegar

1½ cups whole wheat pastry flour

2½ cups unbleached all-purpose flour, plus more for dusting

2 teaspoons baking powder

2 teaspoons fast-rising dry yeast

½ teaspoon baking soda

½ teaspoon sea salt

¼ cup coconut oil

FILLING

¼ cup plus 1 table-spoon coconut oil

⅔ cup coconut sugar

2 teaspoons ground cinnamon

INSTRUCTIONS

1. Preheat the oven to 400°F.
2. To make the rolls: In a small bowl, combine 1½ cups of the nondairy milk and the vinegar and set aside.
3. In a large bowl, whisk together the pastry flour, 1½ cups of the all-purpose flour, the baking powder, yeast, baking soda, and salt.
4. Melt the coconut oil in a small saucepan over medium heat. Once melted, whisk in the milk-vinegar mixture and stir until warmed through (the liquid should be warm to the touch, between 120° and 130°F). Remove from the heat and add to the flour mixture. Stir to combine.
5. Add the remaining 1 cup all-purpose flour and stir well until a soft dough forms (use your hands, if needed).
6. Place the dough on top of a silicone baking mat and, if the dough is sticky, lightly sprinkle more flour on top. Use a rolling pin to roll out the dough into a 10 x 14-inch rectangle. Brush the surface with the remaining 1 tablespoon non-dairy milk.
7. To make the filling: Melt ¼ cup of the coconut oil in a small saucepan over medium-low heat.

FROSTING

⅓ cup coconut sugar

2 tablespoons tapioca flour

1 tablespoon nondairy milk

¼ teaspoon ground cinnamon

¼ teaspoon pure vanilla extract

MAKE IT GLUTEN-FREE:
Replace the whole wheat pastry flour and 1½ cups of the unbleached all-purpose flour with 3 cups Gluten-Free Flour Mix (page 179) plus 2 teaspoons xanthan gum. Replace the remaining 1 cup unbleached all-purpose flour with 1 cup gluten-free oat flour.

8. In a small bowl, combine the melted coconut oil with the coconut sugar and cinnamon. Sprinkle the mixture over the surface of the dough and use the back of a spoon to smooth it out over the entire surface.

9. Starting from the long end, roll the dough into a log. It's helpful to lift up the silicone mat and push it over the dough as you roll to help prevent sticking. Once rolled, be sure the end of the dough is underneath the roll. Using a serrated knife, gently cut the roll in half, and then cut each half into four pieces, for a total of eight pieces.

10. Place the pieces cut-side up in an ungreased 9-inch round pan or pie plate (start with one in the center and place seven more around the edges of the pan). With the palm of your hand, gently press down on each roll.

11. Melt the remaining 1 tablespoon coconut oil and brush it over the top of the rolls.

12. Bake for 25 minutes, until golden brown. Let cool a little before frosting.

13. Meanwhile, to make the frosting: Combine the coconut sugar, tapioca flour, nondairy milk, and cinnamon in a small saucepan. Cook over low heat until the sugar has melted, about 5 minutes. Remove from the heat and whisk in the vanilla.

14. Drizzle the frosting over the cinnamon rolls. Serve immediately, or store the rolls in an airtight container in the fridge for up to 3 days, or freeze for up to 2 months. Reheat in the oven at 350°F for about 5 minutes before serving.

Toaster Pastries

MAKES 8 TO 10 TARTS

Remember those sugary, foil-wrapped Pop-Tarts we all loved as kids? So good, yet so bad. This version is far more satisfying and flavorful. We use our homemade Strawberry Chia Jam for the filling, but you can fill these with just about any jam or spreadable filling you like.

INGREDIENTS

1 cup whole wheat pastry flour

¾ cup unbleached all-purpose flour

1 tablespoon coconut sugar

¼ teaspoon sea salt

½ cup plus 1 tablespoon solid coconut oil (see tip, page 88)

1 teaspoon pure vanilla extract

½ tablespoon apple cider vinegar

About ½ cup Strawberry Chia Jam (page 111) or other jam

Nondairy milk, for brushing

1 recipe Lemon Glaze (recipe follows; optional)

INSTRUCTIONS

1. In a food processor, combine the pastry flour, all-purpose flour, coconut sugar, and salt and pulse until combined.
2. Add the coconut oil and process until thoroughly combined. Add 3 tablespoons water, the vanilla, and the vinegar and process until the dough holds together and starts to form a ball on the blade. If needed, add more water a little at a time (up to 2 tablespoons) and process until the dough holds together.
3. Place the dough on a large piece of parchment paper and shape it into a disc with your hands. Place another piece of parchment paper on top and use a rolling pin to roll from the center out. As you roll out the dough, rotate the paper so you roll in even directions to produce a relatively even 12 x 16-inch rectangle about ⅛ inch thick. Remove the top piece of parchment paper and trim the edges using a pastry cutter or sharp knife.
4. Cut the rectangle into even squares, about 2½ x 2½ inches (you should get 16 to 20 squares total).
5. Place 1 tablespoon of jam in the center of every other square. Top each jam-filled square with a plain square of dough and press the edges gently to seal each of the filled pockets. Use a fork to crimp the edges and gently prick vent holes in the top of each tart.

TIP: Use coconut oil that is in its solid state, similar to cold butter. If you live in a warm environment and your coconut oil is soft, place the whole jar in the fridge for an hour or so before using.

MAKE IT GLUTEN-FREE: Replace the whole wheat pastry flour and all-purpose flour with 1¾ cups Gluten-Free Flour Mix (page 179) plus ½ teaspoon xanthan gum.

6. Transfer the tarts, still on the parchment paper, to a baking sheet and refrigerate for 30 minutes.
7. Preheat the oven to 350°F.
8. Brush the chilled tarts with nondairy milk. Bake for 25 to 30 minutes, until the edges are golden brown. Let cool slightly before serving, and spread with glaze, if desired. Store in an airtight container in the fridge for up to 3 days. (To store for a longer period, freeze unglazed tarts in an airtight container for up to 2 months. Reheat in the oven or toaster oven at 375°F for about 10 minutes. Spread with glaze before serving, if desired.)

Lemon Glaze

INGREDIENTS

¼ cup coconut butter, homemade (page 112) or store-bought, softened

2 tablespoons pure maple syrup

2 tablespoons fresh lemon juice

¼ teaspoon pure vanilla extract

INSTRUCTIONS

In a blender, combine all the ingredients and blend until smooth.

Awesome Energy Bars

. . . .

MAKES 12 BARS

These bars have been my most-requested recipe by all of the obliging taste-testers in my life (family, friends, neighbors, colleagues . . . anyone I could find who was still hungry). I feel like I've made them a million times and a million different ways. When the request for another batch comes in on a busy night, I just mix in the carob or chocolate chips rather than taking the extra time to cool the bars and spread on a smooth carob/chocolate layer. Either way, these are a winner. —L. P.

INGREDIENTS

½ cup raw sunflower seeds

½ cup raw pumpkin seeds

⅓ cup raw almonds

⅓ cup almond butter

¼ cup pure maple syrup

¼ cup brown rice syrup

⅓ cup brown sesame seeds

⅓ cup raw hemp hearts

2 tablespoons flax meal

½ cup carob chips

> **TIP:** These bars are a bit sticky, so use a small piece of parchment paper to press them evenly into the pan without covering your hands in sticky, tasty bar batter.

INSTRUCTIONS

1. Preheat the oven to 350°F. Line an 8 x 8-inch square baking pan with parchment paper.
2. In a food processor, combine the sunflower seeds, pumpkin seeds, and almonds and pulse into a chunky meal.
3. In a medium bowl, stir together the almond butter, maple syrup, and brown rice syrup.
4. Fold in the nut-and-seed meal, sesame seeds, hemp hearts, and flax meal. Stir until well combined.
5. Press the batter into the prepared pan. Bake for 20 minutes. Let cool to room temperature.
6. Melt the carob chips in a double boiler (see instructions on page 32). Pour the carob over the bars and quickly spread it into an even layer with an offset spatula or the back of a spoon. Let cool in the fridge or on the counter until firm, about 20 minutes.
7. Once firm, cut into 12 bars. Store in an airtight container in the fridge for up to 2 weeks or in the freezer for 2 to 3 months.

> **TRY THIS:** The best thing about these bars is you can easily adapt them with your own favorite ingredients. Try them with pecans or pistachios instead of almonds, replace the brown sesame seeds with toasted black sesame seeds, and switch out the carob for chocolate.

Snackworthy Cereal Bars

. . . .

MAKES 10 TO 12 BARS

We packed these easy snack bars with some of our favorite ingredients, but really, this is a pretty customizable recipe—swap out the nuts, seeds, or dried fruit and you have a whole new bar. Tuck one or two in your purse or travel bag for an easy snack when on the go. Or hey, since there are oats and cereal in there, why not bite into one for breakfast?

INGREDIENTS

2 cups puffed brown rice cereal

1 cup rolled oats

½ cup chopped pecans

½ cup dried cranberries

⅓ cup raw pumpkin seeds

¼ cup raw hemp hearts

½ cup coconut sugar

½ cup brown rice syrup

3½ tablespoons coconut oil

¼ teaspoon sea salt

2 teaspoons pure vanilla extract

> **TRY THIS:** For a nut-free version, replace the pecans with ½ cup raw sunflower seeds.

INSTRUCTIONS

1. Line an 8 x 8-inch square baking pan with parchment paper.
2. In a large bowl, combine the puffed rice cereal, oats, pecans, cranberries, pumpkin seeds, and hemp hearts.
3. In a small saucepan, combine the coconut sugar, brown rice syrup, coconut oil, and salt. Bring to a simmer over medium-low heat. Simmer, stirring occasionally, for about 2 minutes, until the sugar has melted and the mixture is smooth and glossy. Remove from the heat and stir in the vanilla.
4. Pour the mixture into the bowl with the dry ingredients and stir to coat. Press into the prepared pan, using a spatula to press down and smooth out the top. Refrigerate for at least 1 hour before cutting into bars. Store in an airtight container at room temperature for up to 1 month.

Nutty Crispy Rice Squares

· ·

MAKES 12 TO 16 SQUARES

I'm going to go out on a limb and assume you're not a fan of the processed junk in the original Rice Krispies treats, yet somehow the great Kellogg's marketing team has been making them a part of kids' lives for generations. They are sticky, sweet, and crunchy, and I still remember shamelessly putting the gooey, cereal-covered mixing spoon straight into my mouth to "taste-test" when I was little. To fulfill the cravings of adults and kids alike, I came up with these crispy rice cereal squares, which are just as I remember but with less sugar, far fewer processed ingredients, and a hint of nutty goodness. If you're anything like me, you'll want to do some taste-testing, too. —N. A.

INGREDIENTS

½ cup Coconut Peanut Butter (page 110)

½ cup brown rice syrup

2 tablespoons coconut sugar

1 teaspoon pure vanilla extract

Pinch of sea salt

3½ cups crispy brown rice cereal

TRY THIS: You can substitute ½ cup of your favorite natural nut butter plus ¼ cup coconut butter for the Coconut Peanut Butter. For a more authentic buttery flavor, try using homemade macadamia nut butter (it's incredible).

INSTRUCTIONS

1. Line an 8 x 8-inch square baking pan with parchment paper.
2. Combine the Coconut Peanut Butter, brown rice syrup, and coconut sugar in a large saucepan. Cook over medium-low heat, stirring occasionally, for 3 to 5 minutes, until melted and smooth. Remove from the heat and stir in the vanilla and salt. Fold in the brown rice cereal and gently stir to coat.
3. Press into the prepared pan, using a spatula to press down and flatten the top. Refrigerate for at least 1 hour before cutting into squares. Store in an airtight container at room temperature for up to 1 month.

Mountain Climber's Mix (page 94)

Mountain Climber's Mix

· ·

MAKES 3½ CUPS

This recipe makes one of the most colorful trail mixes you've ever seen. It takes minutes to throw together and offers a variety of flavors and textures in every handful. Plus, you can get through the security checkpoint—making for a reliable source of energy and nutrition, whether you're climbing to 30,000 feet or to the edge of the Niagara escarpment. Happy hiking!

INGREDIENTS

½ cup raw almonds

½ cup raw cashews

½ cup raw pumpkin seeds

½ cup raisins

½ cup goji berries

½ cup uncrystallized ginger, or ¼ cup crystallized ginger

¼ cup walnuts

¼ cup Brazil nuts

Pinch of sea salt

INSTRUCTIONS

Combine all of the ingredients in a bowl and stir well. Store in an airtight container at room temperature for 2 to 3 months.

TRY THIS: Add chocolate chips or White Chocolate Chips (page 217) to delight kids and kids-at-heart.

Cheesy Crackers

Remember those bright orange cheesy crackers you grew up with? Well, these aren't them. These plant-based, cheddar-flavored crackers are salty and buttery with a hint of onion and oregano. But they're made with the finest finger-licking ingredients we could find—and we bet you won't be able to stop eating them.

INGREDIENTS

½ cup unbleached all-purpose flour

¼ cup whole wheat pastry flour

¼ cup oat flour

2 tablespoons nutritional yeast flakes

½ teaspoon sea salt

¼ teaspoon onion powder

¼ teaspoon dried oregano

¼ teaspoon freshly ground black pepper

⅛ teaspoon turmeric powder

¼ cup solid coconut oil (see tip, page 88)

MAKE IT GLUTEN-FREE: Replace the unbleached all-purpose flour and whole wheat pastry flour with ¾ cup Gluten-Free Flour Mix (page 179). Use oat flour that is certified gluten-free.

INSTRUCTIONS

1. Preheat the oven to 350°F.
2. In a food processor, combine the all-purpose flour, pastry flour, oat flour, nutritional yeast, sea salt, onion powder, oregano, pepper, and turmeric and process until combined.
3. Add the coconut oil and process until combined and no chunks of oil remain.
4. Add 3 tablespoons water and process until a soft dough forms. If needed, add more water a little at a time, up to 2 tablespoons. The dough should just be moist enough to hold together when pressed.
5. Place the dough on a large piece of parchment paper and form it into a rectangle with your hands. Place another piece of paper on top and press down to flatten. Using a rolling pin, roll the dough into a relatively even 10 x 12-inch rectangle, about ⅛ inch thick. Remove the top parchment and trim the edges using a pastry cutter or sharp knife. Cut the dough into squares, about 1 x 1 inch each, leaving them in place on the parchment.
6. Transfer the parchment with the cut dough on it to a baking sheet. Bake for 15 minutes.
7. Remove the pan from the oven and use a fork or knife to carefully (they're hot!) separate the crackers and spread them out so they have more space between them (this will help the middle crackers cook more evenly). Bake for 5 to 8 minutes more, until lightly golden and crisp. Let cool completely. The crackers can be stored in an airtight container at room temperature for about 1 month.

Pecan and Raisin Rice Crackers

MAKES ABOUT 60 CRACKERS

No homemade pantry is complete without crackers. These crispy little gems contain a base of cooked brown rice and flax and are sweetened up with raisins and maple syrup. They are just yum. If this is your first time making your own crackers, don't be nervous. These come together quickly and seamlessly. Just be sure to roll the dough as thin and evenly as possible. You'll have a big batch of delicious, healthy snackables in no time.

INGREDIENTS

½ cup flaxseeds

2¼ cups cooked short-grain brown rice, cooled (from about 1 cup uncooked)

½ teaspoon ground cinnamon

3 tablespoons pure maple syrup

½ cup raisins

½ cup raw sunflower seeds

½ cup chopped pecans

INSTRUCTIONS

1. Preheat the oven to 350°F.
2. In a small bowl, stir together the flaxseeds and ½ cup water and let stand for about 15 minutes, until gelled.
3. In a food processor, combine the flaxseed mixture, brown rice, cinnamon, and maple syrup and process until well combined. Add the raisins, sunflower seeds, and pecans and pulse to combine. You want to leave some chunks for texture. The mixture will be very sticky.
4. Scoop out half the mixture onto a large piece of parchment paper. Top with another piece of parchment and press down to flatten. Use a rolling pin to roll it out into a very thin, even layer, about ⅛ inch thick. Remove the top piece of parchment paper and score the dough into square or diamond-shaped crackers. Transfer the parchment paper, with the crackers on it, to a baking sheet. Roll out the remaining dough using the same process and transfer to a second baking sheet.
5. Bake for 25 minutes. Remove the baking sheets from the oven, lift the parchment paper, and flip the crackers over onto the baking sheets. Carefully peel off and discard the parchment paper. Continue baking for 10 to 15 minutes, until golden brown and dry to the touch. Let cool completely before breaking apart with your hands. Store the crackers in an airtight container at room temperature for about 1 month or in the freezer for up to 3 months.

Super-Seedy Crackers

MAKES ABOUT 50 CRACKERS

These remind us of a very popular brand of gluten-free crackers on the market. Who are we kidding? We painstakingly worked to replicate those crackers because, despite their cost, we couldn't stop popping a box into our shopping basket on each grocery trip. These seedy crackers, studded with pumpkin and sesame seeds, deliver on the flavor and crunchy texture for less than a quarter of the price of the boxed variety. So now they're our new favorite vehicle for hummus, salsa, and baba ghanoush. Huzzah for homemade!

INGREDIENTS

2 cups brown rice flour

¼ cup flax meal

3 tablespoons psyllium husks

Pinch of sea salt

⅓ cup brown sesame seeds

⅓ cup black sesame seeds

⅓ cup raw pumpkin seeds

⅓ cup raw sunflower seeds

3 tablespoons canola oil

1 tablespoon Bragg Liquid Aminos

2 teaspoons toasted sesame oil

TIP: The secret to crunchy homemade crackers is getting the dough spread super thin before baking. But those super-thin crackers can burn if ignored, so watch them closely. If you're baking on two baking sheets at once, switch them from bottom to top spot (and top to bottom) in the oven halfway through.

INSTRUCTIONS

1. Preheat the oven to 400°F.
2. In a medium bowl, combine the brown rice flour, flax meal, psyllium husks, salt, brown and black sesame seeds, pumpkin seeds, and sunflower seeds.
3. In a small bowl, combine the canola oil, liquid aminos, sesame oil, and 2 cups water. Add the wet mixture to the dry mixture and stir until well combined.
4. Divide the dough into quarters. Roll out each quarter between two large pieces of parchment paper (see instructions on page 95). The thinner you roll the dough, the crispier your crackers will be. Once you've achieved the desired thickness, remove the top piece of parchment paper. Score the dough into square crackers, then transfer the parchment paper, with the crackers on it, to a baking sheet. If you're using two baking sheets, roll out and bake the first two batches and then repeat for the last two.
5. Bake each batch for 25 minutes. Flip the crackers, remove the parchment, and continue to bake for 10 minutes more. The crackers should be golden brown. Let cool completely on the baking sheet.
6. Break the crackers apart on the scored lines using a knife, pizza cutter, or your hands. Store in an airtight container at room temperature for up to 1 month or in the freezer for up to 3 months.

Kale Chips

· · · · · · · · · · · · · · · · ·

MAKES 4 CUPS

Believe it or not, this was probably one of the most challenging recipes in the book to create. We have been making kale chips in our dehydrators for years but wanted to create the same crunchy texture in the oven so everyone could enjoy it. We ate a lot of stewed, creamy kale for a while before we figured out the best result would come from a light and simple dressing that really allows the kale to become thin and crispy. So here you go, the ultimate light, healthy snack for chip lovers everywhere.

INGREDIENTS

8 cups curly green kale, washed and dried thoroughly and torn into bite-size pieces

2 tablespoons apple cider vinegar

2 teaspoons olive oil

¼ to ½ teaspoon sea salt

TIP: Make sure the kale is very dry before tossing it with the remaining ingredients. Any remaining dampness can make the chips taste a little bitter. Drying them will also help the chips crisp up rather than stay soggy, which is a pretty essential quality for fantastic chips. These can burn quickly, so watch them *closely*.

INSTRUCTIONS

1. Preheat the oven to 300°F. Line two baking sheets with parchment paper.
2. In a large bowl, toss the kale with the vinegar, oil, and salt until it is evenly coated.
3. Spread the kale into a single layer on the prepared baking sheets.
4. Bake for 25 minutes. Let cool on the baking sheets before serving or transferring to a container. The chips stay crispier if you leave them uncovered. The chips will keep at room temperature for 4 to 5 days.

TRY THIS: Add some cheesiness by tossing in 1 tablespoon nutritional yeast flakes.

Spice It Up Tortilla Chips

· ·

MAKES 48 CHIPS

Next time you have a craving for Doritos, skip past the chip aisle and pick up a package or two of soft corn tortillas instead. Since these spicy baked chips are free of ingredients like Red #40, corn syrup, and MSG, it's okay if you want to eat the whole batch yourself (because you can easily make another).

INGREDIENTS

6 small soft corn tortillas

1 tablespoon olive oil

1 teaspoon garlic powder

1 teaspoon onion powder

1 teaspoon chili powder

½ teaspoon paprika

½ teaspoon chipotle powder (reduce for less heat)

½ teaspoon sea salt

½ teaspoon cane sugar

½ teaspoon nutritional yeast flakes

¼ teaspoon dried oregano

⅛ teaspoon freshly ground black pepper

INSTRUCTIONS

1. Preheat the oven to 425°F. Line two baking sheets with parchment paper.
2. Cut each tortilla into 8 triangles and place them in a large bowl. Drizzle with the olive oil and stir to coat (use your hands if it's easier).
3. In a dry spice grinder or blender, combine the remaining ingredients and pulse until powdered. Sprinkle the spice mixture over the tortillas and mix with your hands to coat.
4. Place the tortillas in a single layer on the prepared baking sheets. Bake for 5 to 7 minutes, flipping the chips halfway through. Let cool before serving (the chips crisp up as they cool). Store in an airtight container at room temperature for up to 1 week.

Sweet Potato Chips

MAKES 4 CUPS

Crunchy, salty chips are so satisfying. But with all the hassle of deep-frying at home, we had basically eliminated them from our diets. When we figured out how to oven-bake chips that were actually crunchy, there was quite a celebration. Fill a bowl with these sweet potato chips and join the party!

INGREDIENTS

4 cups thinly sliced unpeeled sweet potato (we use a mandoline blade set at .75 mm)

2 tablespoons nutritional yeast flakes

1 tablespoon olive oil

1 teaspoon garlic powder

Sea salt, for garnish

TIP: Watch these chips closely while baking. Depending on the thickness of each chip, the baking time can vary. If you have some chips that are thinner than others, pull those out of the oven as soon as they turn brown and crisp up.

INSTRUCTIONS

1. Preheat the oven to 425°F. Line two baking sheets with parchment paper.
2. Dry the sweet potato chips using a paper towel or clean dish towel.
3. In a large bowl, toss the sweet potato with the nutritional yeast, olive oil, and garlic powder until well coated.
4. Working in batches, arrange the slices in a single layer over the prepared baking sheets. Bake the slices for 12 to 14 minutes, until slices are browning and the edges are curling. Depending on your oven, you may want to rotate the trays halfway through the cooking time. Repeat with the remaining sweet potato slices.
5. Remove from the oven, pour the chips into a large bowl, toss each batch with a pinch of salt, and serve.

Coconut Bacon Bits

. . . .

MAKES 2 CUPS

You've just got to give these a try. We love to use them in vegan club sandwiches, in salads, or to coat an amazing Classic Cheese Ball (page 60). But if you're someone who loves smoky, salty sweets, you can also add these as a topping to doughnuts, cookies, and brownies. P.S. One of our testers told us this recipe alone was worth the price of the book.

INGREDIENTS

1 tablespoon tamari

1 tablespoon vegan Worcestershire sauce, homemade (page 139) or store bought

2 teaspoons liquid smoke

2 teaspoons pure maple syrup

2 teaspoons olive oil (optional)

½ teaspoon apple cider vinegar

½ teaspoon smoked paprika

2 cups large coconut flakes

INSTRUCTIONS

1. Preheat the oven to 300°F. Line a baking sheet with parchment paper.
2. In a medium bowl, combine the tamari, Worcestershire, liquid smoke, maple syrup, olive oil (if using), vinegar, and paprika and stir. Toss in the coconut flakes and stir until well coated and no liquid remains at the bottom of the bowl.
3. Spread the coated coconut in a single layer over the prepared baking sheet. Bake for 18 to 20 minutes, stirring every 5 minutes. Watch carefully—the edges can burn quickly! Let cool on the baking sheet. Store in an airtight container at room temperature for up to 1 month.

> **TRY THIS:** If you're looking to reduce your oil consumption, the natural fat in the coconut flakes make these delicious with or without the oil in the recipe. If you like things a little more on the salty side, add a sprinkle of salt once you lay out the coconut flakes on the baking sheet, before they go into the oven.

Crunchy Italian-Seasoned Croutons

MAKES ABOUT 45 CROUTONS

These flourless croutons are packed with so much flavor and goodness, you'll never want to go back to oil-laden bread croutons again. We were inspired to come up with this recipe after trying the croutons from Angela Liddon's book, *The Oh She Glows Cookbook*. Spiked with our homemade Italian Spice Mix and a mix of simple seeds, these croutons are meant to be thrown on salads by the handful.

INGREDIENTS

1½ tablespoons flax meal

1 clove garlic

½ cup raw sunflower seeds

¼ cup raw pumpkin seeds

2 tablespoons raw hemp hearts

2 teaspoons Italian Spice Mix (page 174)

½ tablespoon olive oil

1 teaspoon tamari

¼ teaspoon sea salt

INSTRUCTIONS

1. Preheat the oven to 350°F. Line a baking sheet with parchment paper.
2. In a small bowl, combine the flax meal and 3 tablespoon water and set aside until gelled, about 5 minutes.
3. In a food processor, pulse the garlic until minced. Add the flax mixture, sunflower seeds, pumpkin seeds, hemp hearts, Italian Spice Mix, olive oil, tamari, and salt and process until combined. Don't overprocess; you want to leave some chunks for texture.
4. Drop crouton-size portions of the dough onto the prepared baking sheet. (We like to use a ½-teaspoon measuring spoon to scoop up the dough and drop it onto the prepared baking sheet with the help of a small spoon in the other hand.) Bake for 25 to 30 minutes, or until golden and dry to the touch. Let cool before serving. Store the croutons in an airtight container at room temperature for up to 1 month.

Quick Pickles

. . . .

MAKES 1 QUART

We wanted a four-season solution to your pickle problem, so we use the ubiquitous English cucumber instead of the kirby, which seems to only make cameo appearances during our brief Canadian summers. The brine creates a bright, sour, and very dilly pickle in just twenty-four hours—without any need for a water bath or canning tongs. Since these pickles are already in long, thin slices, they are ideal for slipping into sandwiches, burgers, and wraps.

INGREDIENTS

1 large English cucumber

1 teaspoon dill seeds

1 teaspoon whole peppercorns (multicolored works well but black, white, or pink are fine, too)

2 cloves garlic, peeled and crushed

4 sprigs fresh dill

¾ cup apple cider vinegar

1 tablespoon kosher or pickling salt (see tip)

1 teaspoon cane sugar

INSTRUCTIONS

1. Remove the ends and halve the cucumber crosswise. Using a vegetable peeler, peel off half of the cucumber's skin (alternating peeled and unpeeled sections so you end up with a cucumber with white and green stripes). Slice the cucumber lengthwise into long, thin strips. Discard or snack on the seedy center strips.

2. Stuff the cucumber slices into a quart-size jar and add the dill seeds, peppercorns, garlic, and fresh dill to the jar with the cucumber.

3. In a small saucepan, combine the vinegar, salt, sugar, and ¾ cup water. Bring to a boil over medium-high heat and boil for 2 minutes.

4. Pour the brine over the cucumbers in the jar. Screw on the lid and let cool to room temperature. Refrigerate for 24 hours to develop the flavor. Enjoy over the next 2 weeks in sandwiches, salads, or just on the side.

TIP: It is important to use kosher or pickling salt rather than table salt. Kosher and pickling salts do not contain iodine or anti-caking ingredients, which can make your brine cloudy and soften the cucumbers.

TRY THIS: When those tiny kirby cucumbers are in season, you can use them instead of the English variety. Just replace the English cucumber with 6 to 8 kirbies. They don't need to be peeled and they pickle well when sliced into spears. Or if you're craving dilled cauliflower, green beans, or carrots, replace the cucumbers altogether or make a mixed vegetable jar—just give those firmer veggies a quick blanch before adding them.

Sweet Ginger Stir-Fry Sauce (page 132)

CHAPTER 5

Sensational Spreads and Sauces

. . . .

SAUCES AND SPREADS CAN TRANSFORM a head of lettuce into a gourmet salad, make toast into a meal, and add the pizzazz to a pesto pizza. Truly, learning to create a flavorful sauce in seconds will change your entire eating experience. A plateful of veggies does not provide the same satisfaction as enjoying those same veggies rolled up in rice paper and dipped into a spicy peanut sauce. Because they are such convenient flavor boosters, many of us have the front doors of our refrigerators devoted to jars of sauces and condiments.

Using the recipes we've created, you can easily switch over to made-from-scratch staples and save yourself money and time in the process. It takes way more time to walk or drive to the store for a jar of almond butter (for six to eight dollars) than to toss some almonds in the food processor and dance around your kitchen until it becomes butter (two dollars and no gas money . . . plus exercise!). Get down with DIY—you'll be minimizing costs and maximizing flavor in no time.

Basic Nut Butter

. . . .

MAKES ABOUT 1 CUP

Sure, you probably already know it's pretty easy to make your own nut butter. But if you've never actually made it, you might not quite understand how ridiculously easy it really is. Take some nuts, throw them in a food processor, and go! As the name implies, this is a basic recipe, so feel free to add sweetener or spices if you desire. We've included instructions on how to roast your nuts, but raw or preroasted nuts work just fine, too. Generally, nuts with a higher fat content, like macadamia or walnut, smooth out quite easily without the need to roast them.

Note that, although this is a very simple recipe, you'll need a little patience as the nuts go through various stages on their way to that extra-smooth consistency. Somewhere in the middle, what seemed like perfectly good nut butter will suddenly become a few degrees smoother—this is the stuff nut butter dreams are made of.

INGREDIENTS

1½ cups raw nuts (if using hazelnuts, see tip)

Pinch or two of sea salt

TIP: If using hazelnuts, you'll want to remove the skins after roasting. Place nuts on a clean kitchen towel, wrap up the towel, and rub the nuts together vigorously to remove the skins. You don't have to be too meticulous about this; some skins remaining is okay. Discard the skins and continue with the recipe.

INSTRUCTIONS

1. Preheat the oven to 350°F. Spread the nuts on a rimmed baking sheet and bake until fragrant, 12 to 15 minutes. You can skip this step if you prefer a raw nut butter or are using preroasted nuts.
2. In a food processor, process the nuts until smooth, stopping to scrape down the sides of the bowl as necessary. The nuts will go from powder to paste to (eventually) a thin, smooth butter. Add salt and pulse to combine. Use immediately or store the butter in a mason jar in the fridge for about 4 months.

Super Seed Butter

MAKES 1 CUP

Until my late twenties, I was a steadfast peanut butter girl. That is, until I discovered the delicious, roasted flavor of sunflower seed butter. It is one great-tasting, convenient food. This version, with the addition of flax, hemp, and chia seeds, ups the ante (and essential omega power) of this spread to super-strength status. Just like homemade nut butters, this recipe requires some time in the food processor in order to achieve a super-smooth consistency. Trust us and be patient—the wait will be worth it. —N. A.

INGREDIENTS

1½ cups raw sunflower seeds

2 tablespoons flaxseeds

1 tablespoon raw hemp hearts

1 tablespoon chia seeds

2 tablespoons pure
maple syrup

1 tablespoon coconut oil
or canola oil (optional)

½ teaspoon pure vanilla extract

¾ teaspoon sea salt

INSTRUCTIONS

1. Preheat the oven to 325°F. Line a baking sheet with parchment paper.
2. Combine the sunflower seeds, flaxseeds, hemp seeds, chia seeds, and maple syrup in a bowl and stir until the seeds are coated with the syrup.
3. Spread out the seeds on the prepared baking sheet. Bake for 12 to 15 minutes, tossing them halfway through, until golden brown. Remove from the oven and carefully transfer to a food processor.
4. Process the seeds for about 15 minutes, stopping to scrape down the sides of the bowl when necessary. The seeds will go from powder to paste to (eventually) a thin, smooth butter. If you find that they are getting stuck at the powder or paste stage, add the oil to help get things moving.
5. Once smooth, add the vanilla and salt and process to combine. The butter can be stored in a mason jar in the fridge for about 4 months. It will thicken once refrigerated.

Chocolate Hazelnut Butter (opposite),
Coconut Peanut Butter (page 110), and
Super Seed Butter (page 107)

Chocolate Hazelnut Butter

MAKES ABOUT 1 CUP

Inspired by a popular commercially prepared spread, this thick, creamy, and chocolaty butter will satisfy even the most intense chocolate craving—sans the hydrogenated oil, dairy, and artificial flavor that make up that familiar name brand. Enjoy it on toast, hot oatmeal, muffins, or straight up on a spoon!

INGREDIENTS

1 cup raw hazelnuts

½ cup raw almonds

2 tablespoons pure maple syrup

1½ ounces dairy-free dark chocolate, finely chopped

½ teaspoon pure vanilla extract

¼ teaspoon sea salt

INSTRUCTIONS

1. Preheat the oven to 325°F. Line a rimmed baking sheet with parchment paper.
2. Spread out the hazelnuts and almonds on the prepared baking sheet and bake for 12 to 15 minutes, tossing the nuts halfway through. Remove from the oven and place nuts on a clean kitchen towel (leave the oven on). Wrap up the towel and rub the nuts together vigorously to remove the skins from the hazelnuts. You don't have to be too meticulous about this; some skins remaining is okay.
3. Return the nuts to the lined baking sheet (discard the hazelnut skins) and drizzle the maple syrup over the top. Use a spoon or spatula to stir and coat the nuts with the syrup. Bake for 12 minutes more. Remove from the oven.
4. Transfer the nuts to a food processor and process for about 10 minutes, stopping to scrape down the sides of the bowl as necessary. The nuts will go from powder to paste to (eventually) a thin, smooth butter.
5. Once smooth, add the chocolate, vanilla, and salt and continue to process until the chocolate has melted and is fully incorporated. The butter can be stored in a mason jar in the fridge for about 4 months. It will thicken once refrigerated.

Coconut Peanut Butter

MAKES 1 CUP

We're infatuated with this sweet, smooth, and oh-so-rich spread. Made with only four ingredients, it is a perfect balance of peanut-buttery goodness and coconut bliss that will take your PB on toast to the next level. Be patient when you're processing the coconut; the smoother you get it, the creamier the end result will be.

INGREDIENTS

1 cup unsweetened shredded coconut

1½ cups dry-roasted unseasoned peanuts

2 teaspoons agave nectar or pure maple syrup

¼ teaspoon sea salt

TRY THIS: This is also amazing with dry-roasted almonds instead of peanuts. Give it a try!

INSTRUCTIONS

1. In a food processor, process the shredded coconut until a paste starts to form. This will take about 10 minutes, so be patient. Stop and scrape down the sides of the processor bowl as needed.

2. Once a paste forms, add the peanuts and continue to process until smooth and silky.

3. Add the agave and salt and process to combine. The butter can be stored in a mason jar in the fridge for about 4 months. It will thicken once refrigerated.

Strawberry Chia Jam

This delicious, subtly sweet strawberry jam has a secret weapon: chia! These magical little seeds are used to give the thick, gelatinous texture that typically develops when using pectin, but in a natural, healthier sort of way. And it's super easy to make! You'll be so impressed with the simplicity of this recipe, you'll want to make a batch every week. If you're using frozen berries, be sure to chop them up a little so they cook up quicker.

INGREDIENTS

2½ cups chopped fresh or frozen strawberries

¼ cup coconut or cane sugar

2 tablespoons chia seeds

½ teaspoon pure vanilla extract

¼ teaspoon fresh lemon zest

TRY THIS: Substitute other small or chopped berries like blueberries or raspberries for the strawberries. You may need to mash them down while cooking to help release their juices.

INSTRUCTIONS

1. Combine the strawberries and coconut sugar in a small saucepan. Cook over medium-low heat for 5 minutes, or until the sugar has melted and the strawberries are starting to soften.
2. Add the chia seeds and stir well. Bring to a boil, then reduce the heat to low and simmer for 10 minutes.
3. Remove from the heat and stir in the vanilla and lemon zest. For a less chunky texture, use a fork to mash down some of the strawberries. Store in a mason jar in the fridge for up to 1 month. It will thicken once refrigerated.

Coconut Butter

Coconut lovers, rejoice! This is the easiest thing to make at home and doesn't come with the hefty price tag of the store-bought stuff. Coconut butter is unlike coconut oil—it is made from whole coconut flesh (not just the oil) pureed into a velvety, nutrition-dense spread. The butter will become solid at room temperature, but if you scoop a little into a saucepan over low heat, it will become soft and pliable once more.

INGREDIENTS

3 cups unsweetened shredded coconut

INSTRUCTIONS

In a food processor, process the coconut until thin and smooth, about 10 minutes. The coconut will go from crumbs to paste to a smooth, thin butter. Stop to scrape down the sides of the processor bowl as needed. The butter can be stored in a mason jar at room temperature for 4 to 6 months. It will harden as it cools.

Italian Dressing

MAKES 2 CUPS

Is there a rule that says you must have a bottle of Italian dressing in your fridge? I ask because I feel like I've spent a lot of time reading the labels of Italian dressings at various dinner parties over the past twenty years. And what I learned reading those labels made me pretty disinterested in store-bought dressing. So, I started making my own, and through the years, I've discovered many different uses for Italian dressing: it adds amazing zing to a green salad, creates a flavorful pasta salad, or makes a great marinade to infuse tofu and vegetables with some Mediterranean magic. This is a bright, bold Italian blend that has all the flavor with none of the fillers. —L. P.

INGREDIENTS

1 cup canola oil

½ cup white wine vinegar

¼ cup minced red bell pepper (see tip)

1 tablespoon nutritional yeast flakes

2 teaspoons Dijon mustard

½ teaspoon sea salt

½ teaspoon dried oregano

½ teaspoon dried thyme

¼ teaspoon dried marjoram

¼ teaspoon red pepper flakes

½ teaspoon garlic powder

Pinch of freshly ground black pepper

INSTRUCTIONS

In a medium bowl, whisk together all the ingredients. Store in an airtight jar in the fridge for 3 to 4 weeks. Shake the dressing before using.

> **TIP:** Remove the white membrane of the bell pepper by laying your knife flat against the inside of each quarter and slicing off the top layer. Then go ahead and mince the dark red pepper flesh. It makes for a better flavor and color in the dressing.

Ranch Dressing

· ·

MAKES 1½ CUPS

If you think you're not much of a salad person, this sensational dressing might just change your mind. The secret is to use fresh herbs to get full flavor, so don't skimp on those. Massage this dressing into kale or other greens (or better yet, make the dip version) and you'll wonder how something so creamy and delicious can be good for you.

INGREDIENTS

1 cup unsweetened almond or cashew milk

⅓ cup raw cashews

1 clove garlic

2 tablespoons fresh lemon juice

1 tablespoon chia seeds

1 tablespoon chopped fresh chives

1 tablespoon chopped fresh flat-leaf parsley

2 teaspoons apple cider vinegar

1 teaspoon onion powder

1 teaspoon pure maple syrup

¼ teaspoon sea salt

⅛ teaspoon freshly ground black pepper

INSTRUCTIONS

In a blender, combine all the ingredients and blend until very smooth. The dressing can be stored in a mason jar in the fridge for up to 2 weeks. It will thicken slightly once chilled.

> **TRY THIS:** This recipe can easily be made into a thick ranch dip for serving with chips and crudités. Simply reduce the almond milk to ½ cup and increase the cashews to ⅔ cup. Once blended, chill in the fridge for a few hours before serving.

Caesar Salad Dressing (page 116), Coconut Bacon Bits (page 101), and Crunchy Italian-Seasoned Croutons (page 102)

Caesar Salad Dressing

MAKES ABOUT 1½ CUPS

Ever since going vegan, I haven't been able to find a bottle of Caesar salad dressing that I love (and could eat). This dressing, however, packs all the flavor without the unappealing ingredient list. Cashews are used to add creaminess, while capers and lemon juice add tang. Instead of omitting the authentic anchovy flavor element, umami-rich kelp granules are used to create the deep, savory profile that is often missing from other vegan Caesar recipes. Toss this dressing with crisp, torn romaine lettuce leaves along with Crunchy Italian-Seasoned Croutons (page 102) and Garlic Parmesan Shaker (page 168) for an extraordinary yet guilt-free salad experience. —N. A.

INGREDIENTS

¾ cup raw cashews, soaked in water for 6 hours

2 stalks celery, coarsely chopped

1 clove garlic

1 tablespoon capers

½ teaspoon kelp granules (optional)

¼ teaspoon mustard powder

¼ teaspoon ground white pepper

¼ teaspoon sea salt

¼ cup fresh lemon juice

INSTRUCTIONS

1. Drain and rinse the soaked cashews.
2. In a blender, combine all the ingredients with ½ cup water and blend on high speed until smooth, about 2 minutes. The dressing can be stored in a mason jar in the fridge for up to 2 weeks.

From top right: Healthy Hatha Hummus (page 120), Classic Hummus (page 118), and Sweet Potato Hummus (page 119)

Classic Hummus

. . . .

MAKES ABOUT 2½ CUPS

We assume every vegan has a favorite hummus recipe. We've always loved the homemade stuff until we discovered a store-bought brand that knocked our socks off with its light and creamy texture. It took many delicious attempts, but we finally found a way to re-create it at home—and better yet, it maintains this texture even in the fridge. We think the secret is whipping the lemon juice. Lemon juice . . . you are magic. We love this hummus straight from the food processor, on a cracker, a carrot, or a spoon.

INGREDIENTS

6 tablespoons tahini, homemade (page 128) or store bought

3 tablespoons fresh lemon juice

2 tablespoons canola oil

1 clove garlic (optional)

¾ teaspoon sea salt

½ teaspoon ground cumin

½ teaspoon smoked paprika

1 (19-ounce) can chickpeas, drained and rinsed, or about 2 cups cooked chickpeas

INSTRUCTIONS

1. In a food processor, combine the tahini, lemon juice, canola oil, garlic, salt, cumin, paprika, and 6 tablespoons water and process until perfectly smooth.

2. Add the chickpeas, one-third at a time, processing until well blended after each addition before adding the next. Store the hummus in an airtight container in the fridge for up to 2 weeks.

TIP: If you don't like smoked paprika, swap it out for sweet paprika. Or leave it out entirely.

TRY THIS: While the basic recipe is already an incredible protein-packed staple to have on hand, jazz it up with fresh herbs like parsley or basil. Garnish with the traditional drizzle of olive oil and sprinkle of smoked or sweet paprika.

Sweet Potato Hummus

. . . .

MAKES 3 CUPS

The big hummus debate—what does it take to be called a hummus? With all the incredible bean dip recipes out there, what are the rules? Well, even though the texture and flavor of this dish may surprise, inside is every traditional hummus ingredient you'd expect (plus a number of fun flavor additions). The sweet potato addition boosts the nutrition in this dip with extra beta-carotene and creates a lighter, creamier texture. Sometimes pushing the envelope of what's expected leads to the greatest discoveries.

INGREDIENTS

1 large sweet potato, peeled, cut into chunks, and steamed until soft (about 1 cup)

1 (19-ounce) can chickpeas, drained and rinsed, or about 2 cups cooked chickpeas

¼ cup tahini, homemade (page 128) or store bought

¼ cup fresh lemon juice

1 teaspoon ground cumin

1 teaspoon spicy curry powder

½ teaspoon smoked paprika

½ teaspoon sea salt

Pinch of freshly ground black pepper

INSTRUCTIONS

Combine all the ingredients in a food processor and process until smooth, adding water (about ½ cup) as needed to create a thick dip consistency. Store in an airtight container in the fridge for up to 10 days. The flavor gets even better the day after it's made.

Healthy Hatha Hummus

· ·

MAKES 2½ CUPS

I once won a hum-off with this recipe. A hum-off? Yes, a big, exciting hummus competition. It was an amazing event with tables full of hummus variations, including everything from chocolate chip hummus to a spicy Mexican blend, but in the end this Indian-inspired hummus and I walked home with the trophy. —L. P.

INGREDIENTS

¼ cup raw cashews, soaked in water for 6 hours

1 (19-ounce) can chickpeas, drained and rinsed, or about 2 cups cooked chickpeas

2 teaspoons fresh lemon zest

2 tablespoons fresh lemon juice

2 tablespoons olive oil

2 Medjool dates, pitted and soaked in warm water for about 20 minutes

1 clove garlic, chopped

2 to 3 teaspoons curry paste, homemade (page 175) or a store-bought brand like Pataks, plus more if you like things a little spicier

2 teaspoons ground cumin, plus more for garnish

1 teaspoon garam masala, plus more for garnish

½ teaspoon sea salt

½ teaspoon turmeric powder

Pinch of freshly ground black pepper

Chopped cashews, for garnish

INSTRUCTIONS

1. Drain and rinse the soaked cashews.
2. In a food processor, combine all the ingredients except the chopped cashews and blend until well combined and a thick, creamy dip has formed. Add water (about ¼ cup) a little at a time while you blend.
3. Just before serving, garnish with a sprinkle of cumin and garam masala and a few chopped cashews. (If not serving immediately, wait until ready to serve before adding the garnishes.) Store in an airtight container in the fridge for up to 10 days.

Baba Ghanoush

· ·

MAKES 1½ CUPS

We consider baba ghanoush one of hummus's older cousins. It has a similar creamy texture and is perfect paired with pita and crackers, but the smoky, garlicky flavor tends to appeal more to an adult palate. This dip is a traditional component of many Middle Eastern cuisines, although it is now enjoyed as an appetizer the world over. We especially love that in Paris it is referred to as *caviar d'aubergines*. It is a great addition to your appetizer spread or your picnic basket.

INGREDIENTS

1 medium eggplant

1 tablespoon canola oil

2 cloves garlic, coarsely chopped

3 tablespoons tahini, homemade (page 128) or store bought

2 tablespoons fresh lemon juice

½ teaspoon sea salt

⅛ teaspoon smoked paprika

¼ cup fresh flat-leaf parsley leaves

INSTRUCTIONS

1. Preheat the oven to 400°F. Line a baking sheet with parchment paper.
2. Remove the top leafy stem of the eggplant and halve the eggplant lengthwise. Prick the skin with tines of a fork. Drizzle with the canola oil and rub until the skin and cut sides are lightly coated.
3. Place the eggplant cut side down on the prepared baking sheet. Roast for 45 minutes, until the skin is charred and wrinkled and the inside of the eggplant is very soft and almost gooey. Let cool.
4. Scrape the flesh of the eggplant (discarding the skin) into a food processor. Add the garlic, tahini, lemon juice, salt, and paprika. Process to combine.
5. Add the parsley and pulse until well combined. Store in an airtight container in the fridge for up to 5 days.

Pico de Gallo

. . . .

MAKES ABOUT 2 CUPS

This little treasure is a serious crowd-pleaser that can be blended up in mere minutes and will make you look like a culinary rock star. Serve it alongside any Mexican meal or just a big bowl of tortilla chips (used only as a vehicle for scooping). This is a fairly mild version but you can always add more jalapeños if you like it hot.

INGREDIENTS

2 cups halved grape tomatoes

1 cup chopped plum tomatoes (or ripe mango for a sweet version)

¼ cup minced red onion

2 tablespoons tomato paste

2 tablespoons fresh lime juice

2 tablespoons chopped fresh cilantro

1 tablespoon apple cider vinegar

2 teaspoons minced jalapeño, seeded if less heat is desired

1 clove garlic, minced

1 teaspoon cane sugar

½ teaspoon red pepper flakes

¼ teaspoon sea salt

INSTRUCTIONS

1. In a food processor, combine all the ingredients and pulse until the desired texture is achieved. If you prefer a chunky salsa, don't overprocess.
2. Refrigerate for at least 1 hour to allow the flavors to get to know one another before serving. Store in an airtight container in the fridge for up to 2 weeks.

Pico de Gallo (opposite), Simple Sour Cream (page 44), and Nacho Cheese Sauce (page 136)

Salsa Verde

. . . .

MAKES 1 CUP

I think some of the best recipes come from discovering something in a restaurant or store that is so good, you are driven to discover its secrets. In Toronto, the Kensington Market neighborhood is home to many amazing Latin shops where purveyors serve up arepas, enchiladas, and empanadas of every imaginable flavor. And one little shop has the most incredible salsa verde I've ever tasted—until now. After weeks of pairing them side by side for comparison, the recipe below finally edged out the competition. —L. P.

INGREDIENTS

6 tomatillos, hulled and washed well

2 cloves garlic

2 jalapeños, seeded if less heat is desired

⅓ cup chopped scallions

1 teaspoon distilled white vinegar

½ teaspoon sea salt

2 tablespoons coarsely chopped fresh cilantro

INSTRUCTIONS

1. In a small saucepan, combine the tomatillos with enough water to cover. Simmer over medium heat until the tomatillos have turned a pale green color, about 10 minutes. Tomatillos tend to float, so you may need to flip them over to cook both sides.
2. In a food processor, process the garlic and jalapeños until finely chopped.
3. Add the tomatillos, scallions, vinegar, and salt to the garlic mixture and process into a thick salsa. If you prefer it chunky, don't overprocess.
4. Add the cilantro and pulse until just combined. Store in an airtight container in the fridge for up to 2 weeks.

Herb Tapenade

· ·

MAKES 2 CUPS

Tapenade seems like such a silly word to describe an olive spread, don't you think? It's so easy to make at home, there's no need to spend the extra money on the premade "gourmet" kind. This particular version includes sun-dried tomatoes and a few basic herbs for an extra punch of flavor and texture. It is best made a few hours ahead so the flavors have time to get to know one another. Use it to stuff mushrooms for a delicious appetizer, toss with greens for a weeknight meal, or spread on crackers for an easy afternoon snack.

INGREDIENTS

½ cup chopped sun-dried tomatoes (not oil packed)

1 cup pitted black olives

1 cup pitted green olives

½ cup chopped fresh flat-leaf parsley

2 large cloves garlic

4 teaspoons fresh lemon juice

½ teaspoon celery seeds

½ teaspoon dried basil

½ teaspoon dried oregano

½ teaspoon dried thyme

¼ cup olive oil

INSTRUCTIONS

1. In a small bowl, soak the sun-dried tomatoes in warm water to cover for 15 minutes. Drain.
2. In a food processor, combine the soaked tomatoes, olives, parsley, garlic, lemon juice, celery seed, basil, oregano, and thyme and pulse until coarsely chopped. The tapenade should be slightly chunky; you do not want to puree it.
3. Add the olive oil and pulse quickly to combine. Store in an airtight container in the fridge for up to 2 weeks.

Basil-Spinach Pesto

· ·

MAKES 1 CUP

A nutritious pesto that's thickened with walnuts and a good dose of greens, this stuff is a must on homemade pizza crust (see pages 154 and 157), stirred into pasta, or slathered on roasted squash. Nutritional yeast takes the place of parmesan, but you won't be able to tell the difference. It's that amazing.

INGREDIENTS

2 cups lightly packed chopped fresh basil

1 cup lightly packed chopped fresh spinach

½ cup walnuts

2 tablespoons nutritional yeast flakes

½ teaspoon sea salt

¼ teaspoon freshly ground black pepper

1 large clove garlic, sliced

1 tablespoon fresh lemon juice

¼ cup olive oil

INSTRUCTIONS

1. In a food processor, combine the basil, spinach, walnuts, nutritional yeast, salt, pepper, and garlic and process until coarsely chopped.
2. Add the lemon juice. With the machine running, stream in the olive oil. Process until evenly distributed. This is best used the day it's made. Otherwise, add a thin layer of olive oil on top to keep it from oxidizing, and store in an airtight container in the fridge for up to 1 week.

Pear and Date Chutney

. . . .

MAKES 1½ CUPS

Chutney is one amazing condiment. It provides a sweet and sour Southeast Asian kick to whatever it tops. You can dress up your favorite veggie burger with a spoonful or stick to the classic combination of a spicy samosa and a dollop of chutney.

INGREDIENTS

2 pears, peeled, cored, and chopped

1 apple, peeled, cored, and chopped

1 cup apple cider vinegar

¼ cup finely sliced shallots

¼ cup Medjool dates, pitted and finely chopped

2 tablespoons coconut sugar

1 (1-inch) piece fresh ginger, peeled and minced

½ teaspoon garam masala

¼ teaspoon ground cinnamon

¼ teaspoon red pepper flakes

Pinch of sea salt

Pinch of freshly ground black pepper

INSTRUCTIONS

1. In a large saucepan, combine all the ingredients. Bring to a simmer over medium heat and stir until the sugar has completely dissolved.
2. Simmer for 60 minutes, stirring every 10 minutes. Remove from the heat and let cool. Store in an airtight container in the fridge for 3 to 4 weeks.

Tahini

· · · · · · · · · · · ·

MAKES 1 CUP

There's no need to buy an entire jar of tahini when you can make your own at home in minutes. This versatile paste can be used in a variety of recipes, including Classic Hummus (page 118) and Tahini Sauce (opposite).

INGREDIENTS

2 cups hulled sesame seeds

1 tablespoon canola oil or other neutral oil (optional)

INSTRUCTIONS

1. Heat a large, dry skillet over medium heat. Add the sesame seeds and toast lightly, stirring frequently. As soon as the seeds start to brown, they are done.

2. In a food processor, process the toasted seeds until smooth, about 15 minutes. Stop to scrape down the sides of the processor bowl as needed. If you find they are getting stuck at the powder or paste stage, drizzle in the oil to help get things moving. The tahini can be stored in a mason jar in the fridge for about 4 months.

Tahini Sauce

. . . .

MAKES 1¼ CUPS

While you may associate tahini sauce only with falafel, this protein-rich sauce has many uses in vegan meals. This particular version is simple and nutritious. The earthiness of the fresh parsley makes it particularly good drizzled over steamed vegetables or plain couscous, or massaged into crisp raw kale.

INGREDIENTS

½ cup tahini, homemade (opposite) or store bought

½ cup chopped fresh flat-leaf parsley (or a combination of parsley and cilantro)

¼ cup fresh lemon juice

2 cloves garlic

¼ teaspoon sea salt

INSTRUCTIONS

In a blender, combine all the ingredients with ½ cup water and blend until smooth. Store in a mason jar in the fridge for up to 2 weeks.

Traditional Tomato Sauce

· ·

MAKES 2 CUPS

Can't afford a trip to Tuscany? No problem. Take the time to enjoy the therapeutic powers of stirring a simmering sauce over a couple of hours. Sip some Chianti, play some opera, and enjoy the landscape views in *Under a Tuscan Sun* while your marinara reduces. Both the flavor and the ritual will be your reward. If San Marzano tomatoes are hard to find in your area, you can replace them with other canned whole tomatoes. Once you've tasted your own traditional tomato sauce, you won't be buying those bottled varieties. No one makes it like you.

INGREDIENTS

1 tablespoon olive oil

1 red bell pepper, diced (1 cup)

2 Medjool dates, pitted and chopped

1 teaspoon dried oregano

¼ teaspoon red pepper flakes (optional)

1 (28-ounce) can San Marzano tomatoes (with or without basil)

⅓ cup unsweetened almond milk

½ sweet onion, peeled, not chopped

2 or 3 whole cloves garlic, peeled, not chopped

½ cup fresh basil leaves

Pinch of sea salt

INSTRUCTIONS

1. In a medium saucepan, warm the olive oil over medium heat. Add the bell pepper and dates and sauté for 2 minutes.
2. Add the oregano and red pepper flakes and sauté for 1 minute.
3. Add the tomatoes, almond milk, onion half, and garlic cloves. Bring to a gentle boil.
4. Reduce the heat to low and simmer for 2 hours. Stir occasionally, breaking down the tomatoes each time. In the last 30 minutes, stir in the basil.
5. Remove and discard the onion half and garlic cloves. If a smoother sauce is preferred, pulse the sauce very briefly in a blender. Otherwise, use the sauce immediately or let it cool to room temperature and store in an airtight container in the fridge for up to 10 days.

> **TRY THIS:** If you like your marinara with a little wine, add ½ cup (white and red both work well) in step 3 before bringing the sauce to a boil.

Pizza Sauce

. . . .

MAKES ABOUT 2 CUPS

If you're putting in the extra effort to make your own pizza, let this quick sauce save you a little time. It uses sun-dried tomatoes to add that deep, long-simmered flavor of a traditional marinara. You truly won't believe how rich and robust the flavor can be without the need to babysit it on your stovetop for hours. Since it's raw, it's ideal for pizza and calzones that will warm the sauce in the oven as you bake your crust. For an easy, go-to weekday dinner, top the Spelt Pizza Dough Mix (page 157) with a generous layer of pizza sauce, a few slices of Buffalo Mozzarella (page 54), and some beautifully placed basil leaves.

INGREDIENTS

½ cup sun-dried tomatoes (not packed in oil), soaked for 30 minutes in warm water

1½ cups coarsely chopped plum tomatoes

1 cup seeded and coarsely chopped red bell pepper

1 Medjool date, pitted and coarsely chopped

1 teaspoon olive oil

1 teaspoon dried oregano

½ teaspoon sea salt

¼ teaspoon freshly ground black pepper

2 tablespoons fresh basil leaves

INSTRUCTIONS

1. Drain and rinse the sun-dried tomatoes.
2. In a food processor, combine the sun-dried tomatoes, plum tomatoes, bell peppers, date, olive oil, oregano, salt, and black pepper and process until smooth.
3. Add the basil and pulse to combine. Store in an airtight container in the fridge for up to 2 weeks.

Sweet Ginger Stir-Fry Sauce

One of the easiest ways to increase your vegetable consumption is to add a stir-fry to your weekly meal plan. But pass up the shelf-stable bottles with the ingredient lists you'd rather ignore, and create your own ready-to-go, saucy-sweet ginger goodness. This recipe makes enough sauce for three batches of stir-fry.

INGREDIENTS

⅓ cup Bragg Liquid Aminos or tamari

¼ cup pure maple syrup

2 cloves garlic, minced

2 tablespoons mirin

1 tablespoon finely grated fresh ginger

2 teaspoons blackstrap molasses

2 teaspoons toasted sesame oil

2 teaspoons fresh lime juice

1½ tablespoons arrowroot powder

INSTRUCTIONS

1. Combine all the ingredients, except for the arrowroot powder, with ½ cup of water in a small airtight container. Shake it to mix well. Store in the fridge for up to 2 weeks.

2. When you're ready to make a stir-fry, in a small saucepan, just before you turn on the heat, mix sauce and arrowroot, using ½ tablespoon of arrowroot powder for each ½ cup of sauce. Stir until all the lumps are dissolved. Bring the sauce to a boil over medium heat and cook until it thickens.

3. Sauté your favorite VIPs—very important plants (e.g., mushrooms, bell peppers, broccoli, bok choy, watercress, cashews, mung bean sprouts). Once everything is heated through, pour the sauce over your veggies and stir until everything is coated and glistening in all that goodness. Serve warm.

Spiced Applesauce

. . . .

MAKES 1¾ CUPS

Perfect for lazy days when you're in need of some apple-cinnamon satisfaction in a comforting sort of way, this Spiced Applesauce is like apple pie but a lot easier. Sweet apples like Golden Delicious or Gala nicely complement the spices here, but feel free to use whatever you have on hand.

INGREDIENTS

2 sweet medium apples (like Golden Delicious or Gala), peeled, cored, and cut into cubes

2 tablespoons coconut sugar

½ teaspoon fresh lemon juice

1 teaspoon ground cinnamon

¼ teaspoon freshly grated nutmeg

2 tablespoons white chia seeds

INSTRUCTIONS

1. Combine the apples, coconut sugar, and 1 cup water in a medium saucepan. Bring to a boil over medium-high heat, then reduce the heat to low and simmer for 25 minutes.
2. Remove from the heat and stir in the lemon juice, cinnamon, and nutmeg.
3. Transfer to a blender, add the chia seeds, and blend for a minute or two, until the seeds are pulverized and the sauce is smooth and thick. Let cool. Store in a mason jar in the fridge for up to 1 week.

Thai Peanut Sauce

. . . .

MAKES 2 CUPS

One of my favorite benefits of traveling is learning to make (and getting to taste) the world's diverse cuisines. On a trip to Thailand, I found myself outside a tiny farm just north of Chiang Mai learning to make peanut sauce the truly Thai way, with a mortar and pestle and a lot of muscle. Back at home, missing the bold flavors, I played with the ingredients I could find in my city to create a quick peanut sauce that I wanted to pour on everything. Of course, it pairs well with veggies and rice, but it can also add some zing to a sandwich or wrap, and makes an amazing salad dressing when thinned out. —L. P.

INGREDIENTS

½ cup raw cashews, soaked in water for 6 hours

½ cup chopped seeded tomato

2 Medjool dates, pitted and chopped

1 clove garlic, minced

½ teaspoon grated peeled fresh ginger

¼ cup natural peanut butter

1½ tablespoons tamari

¼ teaspoon cayenne pepper, or 1 minced red Thai chile

1 tablespoon fresh lime juice

TRY THIS: If made in advance, this recipe will thicken as it cools. It can be served as a dip or thinned by whisking in warm water to make it a pourable dressing to toss with noodles or stir-fry.

INSTRUCTIONS

1. Drain and rinse soaked cashews. In a blender, combine the cashews and ½ cup water and blend until completely smooth, stopping to scrape down the sides of the blender jar as needed. Set the cashew cream aside.

2. In a small saucepan, combine the tomato and dates. Cook over medium heat, stirring firmly, for 5 minutes, until a thick paste forms.

3. Add the garlic and ginger and cook for 2 minutes more.

4. Add the peanut butter, tamari, and cayenne. Reduce the heat to low and stir until well combined.

5. Add the cashew cream and lime juice. Stir until well mixed. Serve warm or let cool and store in an airtight container in the fridge for up to 10 days. When reheating, add 1 to 2 tablespoons water to thin the mixture back to a thick, creamy sauce.

Nacho Cheese Sauce

· ·

MAKES 1¾ CUPS

When you're celebrating—be it by watching a big game, marking another Cinco de Mayo, or simply spending a Friday night chatting with your favorite friends, satisfying party food is required. This nacho cheese sauce is a great addition to any festive spread. It is perfect for dipping tortilla chips, drizzling across spicy enchiladas, or adding some creaminess to a special seven-layer dip. Unlike the stuff they serve at the movie theater, we love that this sauce uses navy beans to create the creamy texture and a little bit of sweet potato for that orange hue.

INGREDIENTS

½ cup cooked navy or great northern beans

½ medium sweet potato, peeled, cut into chunks, and steamed until fork-tender (about ½ cup)

¼ cup nutritional yeast flakes

1 tablespoon tahini

1 tablespoon Bragg Liquid Aminos or tamari

1 jalapeño pepper, seeded if less heat is desired

1 teaspoon Mexican chili powder

½ teaspoon ground cumin

Pinch of freshly ground black pepper

Pinch of smoked paprika (optional)

INSTRUCTIONS

In a blender, combine all the ingredients with 2 tablespoons water and blend until completely smooth. Store in an airtight container in the fridge for 10 to 12 days.

> **TIP:** To reheat, place the sauce in a small saucepan over medium-low heat, whisking often, until warmed through, 5 to 7 minutes. Add 2 to 3 teaspoons water to thin out the sauce, if desired.

Sweet & Sour Dipping Sauce

MAKES 1¼ CUPS

This is the only sweet and sour sauce you will ever need, and it makes use of ingredients you probably already have in your pantry. Use it for dipping spring rolls or pouring over steamed veggies, brown rice, or baked tofu—the possibilities are endless.

INGREDIENTS

⅓ cup pure maple syrup

⅓ cup unseasoned rice vinegar

2 tablespoons tamari

1½ tablespoons arrowroot powder or organic cornstarch

1 tablespoon Tomato Ketchup (page 141) or tomato paste

¼ teaspoon toasted sesame oil

¼ teaspoon paprika

INSTRUCTIONS

In a small saucepan, whisk together all the ingredients with ½ cup water. Bring the sauce to a boil over medium heat. Continue to whisk for a minute or two until the sauce has thickened. Remove from the heat and let cool. Store in a mason jar in the fridge for up to 2 weeks.

Fran's Hot Sauce

· ·

MAKES ½ CUP

Fran has the secret recipe for turning up the heat (although she may have got it from her friend Frank). This fermented, vinegar-based hot sauce is fantastic to have on hand. You can add a few drops to spice up your peanut sauce, drip a little into your tacos, or just jazz up your salads with a teeny tiny splash.

INGREDIENTS

4 ounces red serrano chiles, stems removed

2 cloves garlic, coarsely chopped

½ cup distilled white vinegar

1 teaspoon cane sugar

½ teaspoon sea salt

TIP: If you can't find serranos, you can use jalapeños instead. The hot sauce will be bright green instead of bright orange but just as delicious.

INSTRUCTIONS

1. In a food processor, combine the chiles, garlic, and 1 tablespoon water. Pulse into a chunky paste.
2. Transfer the mixture to a small jar with a lid. Ensure the lid is on loosely to allow some gas to escape as the hot sauce ferments. Set aside to ferment on a countertop for 36 hours.
3. Add the vinegar, sugar, and salt. Ferment for 5 days more.
4. Transfer the mixture to a blender and blend until smooth.
5. Press through a fine-mesh sieve into a bowl to remove any remaining seeds or fibers (the end result should be almost watery and a bright orangey-red color). Store in the fridge in an airtight container for 3 to 4 months.

L. P.'s Worcestershire Sauce

MAKES ¾ CUP

This sauce is all about umami—that savory taste that adds a depth, a heartiness, a meatiness to your dishes. Unfortunately, the famous Lea & Perrins Worcestershire uses anchovies to achieve that umami element, so Lisa Pitman had to take on a vegan version. The result is a true staple that can be added to ketchups, barbecue sauces, mushroom dishes, and, of course, Coconut Bacon Bits (page 101) to elevate those rich, robust flavors.

INGREDIENTS

1 cup apple cider vinegar

¼ cup tamari

2 tablespoons pure maple syrup

1 teaspoon black-strap molasses

½ teaspoon ground ginger

½ teaspoon mustard powder

½ teaspoon onion powder

¼ teaspoon garlic powder

¼ teaspoon ground allspice

¼ teaspoon liquid smoke

¼ teaspoon ground white pepper

¼ teaspoon xanthan gum

¼ teaspoon citric acid

Pinch of ground cloves

INSTRUCTIONS

Combine all the ingredients in a small saucepan and whisk well. Bring the mixture to a boil over medium-high heat, then reduce the heat to low and simmer for 20 minutes. The sauce should reduce to about half its original volume and thicken. Let cool for about 20 minutes. Store in an airtight container in the fridge for up to 3 months.

BBQ Sauce

. . . .

MAKES 1¼ CUPS

We love this sauce because of its tangy and peppery elements, and after a night in the fridge, the flavor is superb. Jazz up your summer meals by slathering it on grilled vegetables, baked tofu, or burgers. If you find yourself licking your fingers, it's a sure sign you should make some more.

INGREDIENTS

1 recipe Tomato Ketchup (opposite)

¼ cup apple cider vinegar

¼ cup pure maple syrup

2 teaspoons blackstrap molasses

1 teaspoon Dijon mustard

1 teaspoon onion powder

½ teaspoon freshly ground black pepper

INSTRUCTIONS

Combine all the ingredients with ¼ cup water in a small saucepan. Bring to a boil over medium heat, then reduce the heat to low and simmer, whisking occasionally, for 30 minutes. You'll likely need to whisk more frequently near the end once the sauce has thickened, as it may start splattering. Allow to cool, then store the sauce in a mason jar in the fridge for up to 2 weeks.

Tomato Ketchup

. . . .

MAKES ABOUT 1 CUP

Did you know that most bottled ketchups contain loads of sugar—often in the form of high-fructose corn syrup—and sodium? While it is a necessary condiment in most households, those added ingredients are not. Now you can make your own in just a few simple steps. This version has all the elements of a perfect ketchup—just the right blend of spice, tang, and real tomato flavor—and is sweetened naturally with Medjool dates.

INGREDIENTS

1 cup chopped tomato

3 tablespoons tomato paste

3 Medjool dates, pitted and chopped

1 tablespoon plus 2 teaspoons apple cider vinegar

½ teaspoon onion powder

½ teaspoon sea salt

Pinch of cayenne pepper

INSTRUCTIONS

1. In a small saucepan, combine the chopped tomato, tomato paste, dates, 1 tablespoon of the vinegar, the onion powder, salt, and cayenne and bring to a boil over medium heat. Reduce the heat to low and simmer, stirring frequently, for 5 minutes. Remove from the heat and let cool.
2. Transfer the mixture to a blender and add the remaining 2 teaspoons vinegar. Blend until smooth. Transfer to a mason jar and refrigerate for several hours before serving. Store in the fridge for up to 2 weeks.

From left: Pickle Relish (opposite), Tomato Ketchup (page 141), Maple-Masala Mustard (page 146), Sweet Potato Chips (page 100), and Garlic Cashew Mayonaise (page 145)

Pickle Relish

. . . .

MAKES ABOUT 4 CUPS

If you're a bit of a condiment connoisseur, you probably like to have options. Well, we'd suggest you include this pickle relish in your roster. It has a fantastic, bright flavor that really balances a sweet ketchup and can cut through the creaminess of a rich mayo.

INGREDIENTS

1 cup finely chopped peeled and seeded English cucumber

1 cup finely chopped white onion

1 cup finely chopped green bell pepper

1 cup finely chopped seeded tomato

½ tablespoon pickling or kosher salt

½ cup distilled white vinegar

1 tablespoon cane sugar

1 teaspoon brown rice flour or unbleached all-purpose flour

1 teaspoon turmeric powder

1 teaspoon yellow mustard seeds

1 teaspoon celery seeds

¼ teaspoon curry powder

INSTRUCTIONS

1. In a medium bowl, combine the cucumber, onion, bell pepper, and tomato with the salt. Stir together and let stand for 1 hour.
2. In a medium saucepan, combine the vegetables, vinegar, and cane sugar. Bring to a boil over medium-high heat. Cook for 25 minutes, until the vegetables are tender.
3. Add the flour and spices and continue to boil until the mixture thickens, 5 to 10 minutes.
4. Remove from the heat and let cool. Store in the fridge in an airtight container for 3 to 4 weeks.

Sweet Corn Relish

· ·

MAKES 3¼ CUPS

To me, this condiment captures the taste of summer. Corn, tomatoes, cucumbers—it is basically August in a jar. When I was a kid, there was always a colorful glass jar of corn relish in the fridge. It was pulled out for BBQs, picnics, and parties. When I first went vegan and was trying veggie burgers and veggie dogs for the first time, I would add a generous spoonful of corn relish. It made everything taste familiar and flavorful. —L. P.

INGREDIENTS

1½ cups fresh corn kernels, cut from fresh cobs

1 cup finely chopped tomatoes

1 cup finely chopped red bell pepper

½ cup finely chopped white onion

½ cup finely chopped peeled and seeded English cucumber

½ tablespoon pickling or kosher salt

½ cup distilled white vinegar or apple cider vinegar

1 tablespoon cane sugar

1 teaspoon brown rice flour or unbleached all-purpose flour

1 teaspoon turmeric powder

1 teaspoon yellow mustard seeds

1 teaspoon celery seeds

¼ teaspoon curry powder

INSTRUCTIONS

1. In a medium bowl, combine the corn, tomatoes, bell pepper, onion, and cucumber with the salt. Stir together and let stand for 1 hour.
2. In a medium saucepan, combine the vegetables, vinegar, and cane sugar. Bring to a boil over medium-high heat. Cook for 20 minutes, until the vegetables are tender.
3. Add the flour and spices and continue to boil until the mixture thickens, 5 to 10 minutes.
4. Remove from the heat and let cool. Store in the fridge in an airtight container for 3 to 4 weeks.

> **TIP:** If you only have frozen corn, add it just before you add the flour and spices.

Garlic Cashew Mayonnaise

These days, there are a number of different vegan mayo alternatives on the market. But depending on where you live, they can be pricey or hard to find—and all come with quite an ingredient list. Making your own mayo means you can satisfy your craving for a creamy, garlicky spread at a moment's notice. We like to slather this garlicky goodness on veggie burgers, use it as a dip for sweet potato fries, or stir it in to add that perfect tanginess to a delicious broccoli salad.

INGREDIENTS

1 cup cashews, soaked in water for 6 hours

1 clove garlic

4 teaspoons fresh lemon juice

2 teaspoons Dijon mustard

1 teaspoon ground chia seeds, preferably white chia

½ teaspoon sea salt

INSTRUCTIONS

1. Drain and rinse the soaked cashews.
2. In a blender, combine the soaked cashews, ½ cup water, the garlic, lemon juice, Dijon mustard, chia seeds, and salt. Blend until smooth. If needed, add up to 2 tablespoons additional water to reach a smooth consistency. Store in an airtight container in the fridge for 10 to 12 days.

TRY THIS: Add your favorite herb—we particularly like this recipe with 1 tablespoon fresh dill.

Maple-Masala Mustard

· ·

MAKES ABOUT 1 CUP

So, let's say you're kind of fancy. Making your own mustard can only raise your culinary cred. The best part is there's actually very little work involved—but everyone will be impressed when you place your homemade spread on the condiment tray. You could even add a little label that says *moutarde*, because using French makes everything fancier. The joy of making your own condiments means you are free to play with the traditional flavors. This maple masala balances the sharp mustard flavor with a lovely spicy sweetness.

Note: You will need to plan ahead to pull this off—it takes a couple of days of soaking those mustard seeds to get a nice smooth spread. We use yellow mustard seeds because they pack quite a powerful flavor punch; the brown ones are even more intense, so be careful if you decide to use those instead (or even a mixture of the two).

INGREDIENTS

⅓ cup yellow mustard seeds

⅓ cup apple cider vinegar

2 tablespoons pure maple syrup

1 teaspoon turmeric powder

¼ teaspoon sea salt

2 teaspoons curry spice blend (we prefer a Madras masala blend)

INSTRUCTIONS

1. In a glass jar or container, combine the mustard seeds, vinegar, ⅓ cup water, the maple syrup, turmeric, and salt. Let stand at room temperature for 48 hours.
2. Transfer the mixture to a blender and blend on high speed, adding 2 tablespoons more water to reach a smooth consistency. If you have a mortar and pestle, grind the mustard seed mixture before adding it to the blender. Add the curry spice and blend again until completely incorporated.
3. Let the finished mustard rest for about 2 weeks in the fridge before serving to allow the flavor to mellow. Store in the fridge for up to 2 months.

Savory Egg Mix (page 163) and
Fran's Hot Sauce (page 138)

CHAPTER 6

Make Your Own Mixes

· ·

WITH THIS CHAPTER, we hope to inspire you to create your own ready-made mixes. If you're looking for ways to save money on your grocery bill, this is the place to start. Not only are homemade mixes more economical than buying them premade at the store, but they can save you money by encouraging you to eat at home. If you have Pancake Mix (page 151) already made or Spelt Pizza Dough Mix (page 157) in the fridge, you'll have fewer excuses to go out for breakfast or order pizza from the local pizza parlor.

Taking a little time over the weekend or on a weekday evening to mix together the dry ingredients for Mac & Cheese Sauce Mix (page 159), Shake & Bake Herb Breading (page 164), or Homestyle Banana-Walnut Muffin Mix (page 180) will cut your prep time in half and make cooking and baking from scratch a breeze. Or try making your own spice blends and fresh curry mixes to have on hand for easy weeknight meals. With a little organization, some tightly sealed mason jars, and stick-on labels, you can have a pantry full of fabulous mixes in no time.

Pancake Mix

· · · · · · · · · · · · · · · · · ·

MAKES ENOUGH MIX FOR 10 TO 12 SMALL (4-INCH) PANCAKES

A stack of warm, whole-grain pancakes drizzled with sweet syrup and piled high with fresh berries is heaven, but vegan and gluten-free pancakes can be tricky to make. We tried countless ideas with unsatisfying results until, on a whim, we added almonds and chia to the mix. This created a pancake that is light in texture but holds together well, and we've made them countless times since. Skip the store-bought mix and instead blitz these simple ingredients in your blender so you have a quick mix on hand for mornings that call for something special. (Recipe to make the pancakes follows.)

INGREDIENTS

1 cup rolled oats

½ cup raw millet

½ cup raw almonds

1 tablespoon chia seeds

1½ teaspoons baking powder

¼ teaspoon ground cinnamon

INSTRUCTIONS

In a dry blender, combine all the ingredients and blend into a fine flour. Store in an airtight container for up to 6 months.

Pancakes

. . . .

MAKES 10 TO 12 SMALL (4-INCH) PANCAKES

INGREDIENTS

1 recipe Pancake Mix (page 151)

1½ cups vanilla nondairy milk

3 tablespoons pure maple syrup, plus more for serving

Coconut oil, for the pan

TRY THIS: Feeling fancy? Add small blueberries (fresh or frozen), thinly sliced banana, or chocolate chips! Once you've poured the batter into the pan, sprinkle some on top and continue to cook.

INSTRUCTIONS

1. In a blender, combine the Pancake Mix, nondairy milk, and maple syrup and blend.

2. Heat a skillet over medium-high heat and lightly grease the pan with coconut oil. Allow the pan to heat up for a few minutes (you'll know it's ready when a drop of water sizzles on the surface of the pan) and then reduce the heat to medium or medium-low. Pour small amounts of the pancake batter onto the pan, forming 4-inch circles. Cook for 2 to 3 minutes, until small bubbles appear on the surface and the edges look dry. Flip the pancakes and lightly cook the other side, for about 1 minute. Transfer to a plate and cover with a clean kitchen towel to keep warm. Repeat until you have used all the batter. Serve immediately with maple syrup.

Chai Concentrate

. . . .

MAKES 2½ TO 3 CUPS CONCENTRATE

The smell of this concentrate as it reduces on the stovetop transports me back to my very first night in India. I arrived there to spend five weeks teaching cooking classes (an incredible and very-far-outside-my-comfort-zone adventure). After an endless long-haul flight, I was greeted outside of the Chennai airport by thousands of people waiting for their loved ones, and luckily one taxi driver looking for me. For three hours, we drove through monsoon rains, and I slipped in and out of consciousness as we careened along the dark rural roads. At one point, we pulled over so the driver could have a cup of chai. For the rest of that drive, my dreams were infused with the aromas of ginger, vanilla, cardamom, nutmeg, and cinnamon. That smell is forever tied in my mind with a sense of calm and an ongoing urge for adventure. —L. P.

INGREDIENTS

⅓ cup agave nectar

1 (1-inch) piece fresh ginger, peeled and thinly sliced

10 green cardamom pods, crushed with your palm or the bottom of a can

8 whole cloves

3 star anise

2 cinnamon sticks, or 1 teaspoon ground cinnamon

1 teaspoon vanilla bean powder, or 1 vanilla bean, halved lengthwise and seeds scraped

¼ teaspoon ground white pepper

⅛ teaspoon freshly grated nutmeg

5 black tea bags

Nondairy milk, for serving

INSTRUCTIONS

1. In a medium saucepan, combine the agave, ginger, cardamom pods, cloves, star anise, cinnamon, vanilla, white pepper, nutmeg, and 5 cups water. Bring to a boil over medium-high heat.
2. Reduce the heat to low and simmer for 60 to 90 minutes. The liquid should reduce by half its volume.
3. Remove from the heat and add the tea bags. Steep for 10 to 15 minutes.
4. Strain the liquid, discarding the solids, and store in a glass jar in the fridge for up to 2 weeks.
5. To serve, combine equal parts chai concentrate and warm nondairy milk. Whisking both together in a small pan over medium heat is ideal.

Gluten-Free Pizza Dough Mix

MAKES ENOUGH MIX FOR 1 LARGE PIZZA OR 2 SMALL THIN-CRUST PIZZAS

This quick mix makes a light, crispy, delicious pizza crust and is specifically designed for those sensitive to wheat or gluten. Use this mix for the Gluten-Free Pizza on page 155. Delightfully easier to work with than traditional dough, this pizza crust is a no-knead, no-nonsense kind of recipe that is ideal for those hectic days when your family is begging for pizza—pronto. Load it with your favorite toppings and savor how delicious homemade pizza crust can be.

INGREDIENTS

1 cup brown rice flour

1 cup quinoa flour

1 cup tapioca flour

1 tablespoon fast-rising dry yeast

1 teaspoon sea salt

½ teaspoon xanthan gum

½ teaspoon baking powder

INSTRUCTIONS

In a large bowl, whisk together all ingredients. Store in an airtight container in a cool, dry place for up to 6 months (or until the "best before" date of the yeast you used).

Gluten-Free Pizza

. . . .

MAKES 1 LARGE PIZZA OR 2 SMALL THIN-CRUST PIZZAS

INGREDIENTS

Cornmeal, for dusting
(optional)

Olive oil, for greasing (optional)

1 recipe Gluten-Free Pizza
Dough Mix (page 154)

1 tablespoon olive oil

Brown rice flour, for dusting

Pizza Sauce (page 131) or
Basil-Spinach Pesto (page 126)

Additional toppings
of your choice

INSTRUCTIONS

1. Preheat the oven to 350°F. Dust a pizza stone or large round baking pan with cornmeal or brush lightly with oil.
2. In a large bowl, combine the pizza dough mix with 1¼ cups warm water (110° to 120°F) and the olive oil. Stir with a wooden spoon until it comes together into a soft dough.
3. Transfer the dough to the prepared pizza stone or pan. Using your hands, work from the center and push to flatten and spread out the dough to the edges of the stone. If the dough is sticky, sprinkle on some brown rice flour while you work it out.
4. Prebake the pizza crust for 25 to 30 minutes, or until it begins to look dry and slightly cracked on top.
5. Remove from the oven and spread generously with Pizza Sauce or Basil-Spinach Pesto and any desired toppings. Return to the oven and bake for 15 minutes more, or until the edges are golden and the toppings are warmed through. Slice and serve immediately.

Spelt Pizza Dough Mix (opposite),
Pizza Sauce (page 131), and Buffalo
Mozzarella (page 54)

Spelt Pizza Dough Mix

- -

MAKES ENOUGH MIX FOR 1 EXTRA-LARGE OR 2 SMALLER PIZZAS

In order to make a great pizza, you need a great crust. Spelt is our flour of choice for natural, wholesome dough—long gone are the days of premade white crust loaded with unhealthy ingredients. Spelt is higher in protein and fiber and has a wonderful nutty flavor and texture. Use this mix for the Spelt Dough Pizza on page 158. Note that spelt isn't gluten-free, so if you're looking for a GF alternative, check out the recipe on page 150.

INGREDIENTS

2 cups spelt flour

1 cup unbleached all-purpose flour

2 teaspoons coconut sugar or cane sugar

2 teaspoons fast-rising dry yeast

1 teaspoon sea salt

INSTRUCTIONS

In a large bowl, whisk together all the ingredients. Store in an airtight container in a cool, dry place for up to 6 months (or until the "best before" date of the yeast you used).

Spelt Dough Pizza

· ·

MAKES 1 EXTRA-LARGE OR 2 SMALLER PIZZAS

INGREDIENTS

1 recipe Spelt Pizza
Dough Mix (page 157)

2 tablespoons olive oil,
plus more as needed

Cornmeal, for dusting
(optional)

Unbleached all-purpose
flour, for dusting

Pizza Sauce (page 131) or
Basil-Spinach Pesto (page 126)

Additional toppings
of your choice

MAKE IT GLUTEN-FREE:
Try the Gluten-Free Pizza
Dough Mix on page 154.

INSTRUCTIONS

1. In a large bowl, combine the pizza dough mix
   with 1¼ warm water (110° to 120°F) and the olive
   oil. Stir with a wooden spoon until the mixture
   comes together into a soft dough.
2. Cover the bowl with a clean kitchen towel and
   set aside in a warm place to rise for 2 to 3 hours
   (or up to 5 hours).
3. Preheat the oven to 425°F. Dust a large pizza
   stone or round baking pan with cornmeal or
   brush lightly with oil.
4. Gently knead the dough into a ball and transfer
   it to the prepared pizza stone or pan. Sprinkle
   the dough with all-purpose flour and use a rolling pin to roll from the center out to the edges
   of the stone or pan. Spread with Pizza Sauce or
   Basil-Spinach Pesto and any desired toppings.
   Bake for 10 to 15 minutes, until the edges are
   golden and puffy and the toppings are warmed
   through. Slice and serve immediately.

Mac & Cheese Sauce Mix

· ·

MAKES ENOUGH FOR 2½ CUPS SAUCE, 4 TO 6 SERVINGS MAC & CHEESE

Just as easy as ripping open a packet of orange powder, this simple mac and cheese sauce mix will make a quick task of getting a family-friendly meal on the table. Nutritional yeast and maca powder are essential to creating the cheeselike flavor and can be easily found at most bulk and health food stores. Use this for the Mac & Cheese on page 161. If you're used to the traditional processed stuff, give yourself a little time to get used to the new flavor and you might find yourself hopelessly addicted, like many others before you.

INGREDIENTS

½ cup nutritional yeast flakes

3 tablespoons arrowroot powder

1 tablespoon maca powder

1 teaspoon mustard powder

1 teaspoon onion powder

1 teaspoon garlic powder

½ teaspoon sea salt

¼ teaspoon paprika

⅛ teaspoon lemon pepper or freshly ground black pepper

For extra kick: ¼ teaspoon chili powder and a pinch of cayenne pepper

INSTRUCTIONS

In a dry blender, combine all the ingredients and blend into a fine powder. Store in an airtight container at room temperature for up to 6 months.

Mac & Cheese

. . . .

SERVES 4 TO 6

INGREDIENTS

1 recipe Mac & Cheese
Sauce Mix (page 159)

2 cups unsweetened
nondairy milk

2 tablespoons olive oil

14-ounce package macaroni
pasta, cooked

INSTRUCTIONS

1. In a blender, combine the cheese sauce mix with
   the nondairy milk and olive oil and blend until
   smooth.
2. Pour the sauce into a medium saucepan and
   bring to a boil over medium heat. Reduce the
   heat to low and simmer, whisking continuously,
   for 1 minute, until thickened.
3. Pour the sauce over the cooked pasta, stir to
   coat, and serve!

TIP: The sauce cooks very quickly, so it's best to get your pasta started first. Once your pasta is almost done, get the sauce going.

TRY THIS: This mac and cheese is also fantastic topped with breading and baked. Scoop the mac and cheese into an 8-inch casserole dish and sprinkle with Shake & Bake Herb Breading (page 164) or fine whole-grain bread crumbs. Bake, covered, at 350°F for about 10 minutes. Remove the cover and broil until browned on top, about 2 minutes.

Savory Egg Mix

MAKES ABOUT 2 CUPS

Here's a secret we're excited to share: a savory egg mix that will transform your tofu scramble, French toast, and quiches. The black salt will give your dishes that distinct eggy smell and taste. We've balanced it out with a healthy helping of nutritional yeast and a blend of starches to mimic eggs' binding ability. Breakfast will never be the same.

INGREDIENTS

1 cup nutritional yeast flakes

½ cup potato starch
(not potato flour)

6 tablespoons tapioca starch

1 teaspoon baking powder

1 teaspoon baking soda

½ teaspoon sea salt

½ teaspoon black salt
(*kala namak*)

Pinch of turmeric powder

INSTRUCTIONS

In a medium bowl, whisk together all the ingredients. Store in an airtight container at room temperature for up to 6 months.

TRY THIS: *Make an amazing tofu scramble:*

In a saucepan over medium heat, heat 2 teaspoons olive oil over medium heat, then add ½ onion, minced, ½ cup chopped mushrooms, ¼ cup chopped tomatoes, and 1 cup crumbled firm tofu and sauté.

Whisk together 2 tablespoons Savory Egg Mix with 2 tablespoons water. Once the tofu scramble is cooked, add the egg mixture and cook until warmed through and all the liquid has been absorbed.

Use up your leftover scramble to make a mind-blowing breakfast burrito, with spicy black beans, salsa, and slices of avocado.

Make French toast for two:

In a blender, combine 1 cup almond milk, 2 tablespoons Savory Egg Mix, 1 tablespoon chia seeds, and ¼ teaspoon ground cinnamon. Blend on high speed until the chia seeds are broken down, about 1 minute. Pour the mixture into a large, shallow bowl. Add a slice of bread to the bowl, cover it with the mixture, and flip it over to cover the other side. Allow it to soak while you heat up a cast-iron pan or skillet (brushed with coconut oil) over high heat. You'll know the pan is hot enough when you drop some water on the surface and it sizzles. Reduce heat to medium. Place soaked bread on the pan and cook, covered, for about 5 minutes, or until browned and no longer sticking to the pan. Flip and cook on the other side. While it is cooking, place another dry slice of bread in the bowl to soak. Repeat the process with another 2 or 3 slices of bread or until the liquid mixture is used up. Serve with maple syrup.

Shake & Bake Herb Breading

MAKES ½ CUP

Yes, this is exactly what you're thinking—a gluten-free, herb-and-spice solution for all your coating needs. If you've been missing that "shake, shake, shake" dance with a sandwich bag, well, we're bringing it back. This takes seconds to prepare and its uses are pretty exciting: you can coat tofu, sliced potatoes, and vegetables like cauliflower, or sprinkle it on top of your next brilliant batch of mac and cheese (see page 161).

INGREDIENTS

½ cup almonds,
ground into a meal

1 tablespoon dried oregano

2 teaspoons garlic powder

1 teaspoon onion powder

½ teaspoon smoked paprika

¼ teaspoon freshly
ground black pepper

INSTRUCTIONS

Combine all the ingredients in an airtight container. Store at room temperature for up to 2 months.

TRY THIS: This is a great coating for tofu. Just dredge slices of tofu in a mixture of olive oil and tamari (1:3 ratio). Then coat each slice with the shake-and-bake mix. Preheat the oven to 350°F. Bake the slices on a parchment paper–lined baking sheet for 30 minutes. Serve with a marinara sauce or dip alongside.

Dill Pickle Popcorn Shaker

Dill-icious! Dill-ightful! Dill-ectable!? If you have stood solemnly staring at the ingredients on any of those movie-theater popcorn seasoning shakers, now is the time to rejoice. This stuff is spectacular. Sprinkle generously on a big bowl of hot popcorn and your taste buds will be singing—but quietly, because there's a movie on.

INGREDIENTS

1 tablespoon dried dill

1½ teaspoons garlic powder

1 teaspoon coriander seeds

1 teaspoon onion powder

½ teaspoon mustard seeds

½ teaspoon cane sugar

¼ teaspoon citric acid

INSTRUCTIONS

In a clean spice grinder, combine all the ingredients and grind to a fine powder. Store in a small spice jar at room temperature for up to 6 months.

Popcorn

MAKES ABOUT 6 CUPS

INGREDIENTS

1 tablespoon coconut oil

⅓ cup popcorn kernels

2 tablespoons melted vegan butter or oil (optional, but recommended)

Popcorn Shaker of choice

INSTRUCTIONS

1. Melt the coconut oil in a large pot over high heat. Add the popcorn kernels and cover. Move the pot around on the burner until the sound of popcorn popping slows.
2. Pour the popcorn into a large bowl. Drizzle with the melted vegan butter and toss with a few teaspoons of the spice blend.

Sour Cream & Onion Popcorn Shaker

MAKES ABOUT ¼ CUP

Tonight may be the night to curl up on the couch with your sweetie and an enormous bowl of popcorn, shaken with enough of this sour cream and onion flavoring to coat your fingers with each bite. We prefer popcorn made in a pot on the stove (see page 166), but if you have an air popper, feel free to use it.

INGREDIENTS

2 tablespoons raw cashews or almonds

1½ teaspoons onion powder

½ teaspoon garlic powder

½ teaspoon dried parsley

½ teaspoon cane sugar

¼ teaspoon sea salt

⅛ teaspoon citric acid

INSTRUCTIONS

In a high-speed blender or clean spice grinder, combine all the ingredients and pulse into a fine powder. Store in a spice jar at room temperature for up to 6 months.

Garlic Parmesan Shaker

MAKES ¼ CUP

Once you taste this, you may wonder why it took you so long to discover the recipe. Save some time by making a double batch in your blender, since you'll end up using it every chance you get. Try it on any pasta dish, Caesar salad, or steamed veggies. This stuff is so good, you won't even miss the dairy.

INGREDIENTS

2 tablespoons raw almonds

2 tablespoons nutritional yeast flakes

⅛ teaspoon garlic powder

⅛ teaspoon sea salt

INSTRUCTIONS

In a high-speed blender or clean spice grinder, combine all the ingredients and pulse until powdered. Store in a small jar at room temperature for up to 6 months.

French Onion Dip Mix

MAKES ABOUT 3 TABLESPOONS

Forget those little packets of dip mixes you see at the store. Have you ever looked at the ingredients list? It can be scary. Instead, combine these simple ingredients for a mix you can have on hand for impromptu guests, and then follow our suggestion to make a delicious dip (see opposite), or feel free make up your own!

INGREDIENTS

2 tablespoons dried onion flakes

1 teaspoon dried parsley

½ teaspoon garlic granules

½ teaspoon sea salt

¼ teaspoon freshly ground black pepper

INSTRUCTIONS

Combine all the ingredients in an airtight container. Store at room temperature for up to 6 months.

French Onion Dip

MAKES ABOUT 2 CUPS

INGREDIENTS

1 recipe Simple Sour Cream (page 44) or 1½ cups store-bought vegan sour cream

1 cup chopped fresh spinach

1½ tablespoons French Onion Dip Mix (opposite), plus more as needed

INSTRUCTIONS

1. Combine the sour cream, spinach, and French Onion Dip Mix in a food processor. Pulse a few times just to incorporate. It's nice to leave some texture; you don't want it completely smooth.
2. Taste and add more dip mix if a stronger flavor is desired. Refrigerate for at least 1 hour before serving.

Superfood Salad Booster

MAKES ABOUT 1 CUP

Calling salad lovers everywhere! Elevate the nutrition, flavor, and texture of any bowl of greens with a crunchy salad topper. Just mix together this combo of healthful seeds, mineral-dense seaweed, savory herbs, and zesty spices. A little sprinkle means a whole lot!

INGREDIENTS

¼ cup puffed quinoa

2 tablespoons sunflower seeds

2 tablespoons pumpkin seeds

2 tablespoons hemp hearts

2 tablespoons sesame seeds

2 tablespoons sliced almonds

2 tablespoons goji berries

½ teaspoon sea salt

¼ teaspoon kelp granules

¼ teaspoon dried dill

⅛ teaspoon lemon pepper or freshly ground black pepper

Pinch of cayenne pepper

INSTRUCTIONS

Combine all ingredients in an airtight container. Store at room temperature for up to 6 months.

Pumpkin Pie Spice Mix

. . . .

MAKES ABOUT 3 TABLESPOONS

Seriously, are you going to pay extra for someone else to stir your spices? We didn't think so. Make your own in seconds, make some for your friends, start a business selling your own spice-stirring services. And then eat pie.

INGREDIENTS

4 teaspoons ground cinnamon

2 teaspoons ground ginger

1 teaspoon freshly grated nutmeg

1 teaspoon ground allspice

½ teaspoon ground cloves

INSTRUCTIONS

Combine all the ingredients in an airtight container. Store at room temperature for up to 6 months.

Canadian Spice Mix

. . . .

MAKES ABOUT 2 TABLESPOONS

There is an Italian Spice, Cajun Spice, Chinese Five-Spice, and so on, but what about Canada? Being a bit biased, we felt this oversight needed to be corrected. So, we present the Canadian Spice—a sweet and savory blend of maple, mustard, and garlic. Although probably less known than our prowess for hockey and love for Tim Horton's coffee, Canadians produce more mustard seed than any country in the world. This blend is a wonderful addition to roasted vegetables, potatoes, sauces, dressings, and popcorn.

INGREDIENTS

1 tablespoon maple sugar

1 teaspoon yellow mustard seeds

½ teaspoon garlic powder

½ teaspoon sea salt

INSTRUCTIONS

In a spice grinder or with mortar and pestle, combine all the ingredients and grind well. Store in an airtight container for up to 6 months.

Chai Spice Mix

MAKES ABOUT 2 TABLESPOONS

Want to create your own chai lattes or add a spicy kick to cookies, pound cakes, and pastries? All you need is a spoon and a few special spices.

INGREDIENTS

1 teaspoon ground ginger

1 teaspoon vanilla bean powder

½ teaspoon ground cinnamon

½ teaspoon ground cardamom

½ teaspoon freshly grated nutmeg

Pinch of ground cloves

Pinch of ground white pepper

INSTRUCTIONS

Combine all the ingredients in an airtight container. Store at room temperature for up to 6 months.

Clockwise from top left: Italian Spice Mix (page 174), Pumpkin Pie Spice (page 170), Canadian Spice Mix (page 170), Taco Seasoning (opposite), and Chai Spice Mix (page 171)

Taco Seasoning

· ·

MAKES ¼ CUP

It's taco night! Break out your best spices and take a DIY approach by mixing together this blend of Mexican must-haves. The best part about making your own seasoning is that you can customize it to suit your tastes. Need a little less heat? Omit the chipotle powder. Once you try this mix, you'll never go back to those premade packets again.

INGREDIENTS

1 tablespoon chili powder

2 teaspoons onion powder

2 teaspoons garlic powder

1 teaspoon paprika

1 teaspoon sea salt

1 teaspoon cane sugar

½ teaspoon dried oregano

¼ teaspoon freshly ground black pepper

¼ teaspoon chipotle powder (optional)

INSTRUCTIONS

In a spice grinder, combine all the ingredients and pulse until powdered. Store in an airtight container at room temperature for up to 6 months.

Italian Spice Mix

MAKES ABOUT ¼ CUP

This blend of dried herbs is a quick and convenient way to add flavor to traditional Italian dishes like lasagna and marinara sauce. Sure, you can buy a premade mix at the grocery store, but why spend the extra money when you can make it yourself? We buy dried herbs at our local bulk-food store so we can whip up this mix in a jiffy.

INGREDIENTS

1 tablespoon dried basil

1 tablespoon dried oregano

1 teaspoon garlic granules

½ teaspoon dried thyme

½ teaspoon dried rosemary

½ teaspoon dried marjoram

INSTRUCTIONS

Combine all ingredients in an airtight container. Store at room temperature for up to 6 months.

Indian Curry Paste Mix

· ·

MAKES ABOUT ¾ CUP

Indian food is an amazing option for vegans—legume-rich dishes covered in bold, spicy sauces. With a great paste as your spice base, quick curries can easily become a weekly staple. Instead of squinting at the ingredient list on the side of the premade curry pastes, make your own. It only takes a couple of minutes and saves you from worrying about preservatives and "natural flavors." This paste is ideal for tomato-based Indian dishes like red lentil dhal or chana masala. Just stir in 2 tablespoons of curry paste as you sauté the onions to create your favorite, flavorful Indian menu in minutes.

INGREDIENTS

2 cloves garlic, minced

1 (2-inch) piece fresh ginger, peeled and minced
(about ¼ cup)

2 teaspoons smoked paprika

2 teaspoons garam masala

1 teaspoon cumin seeds

1 teaspoon coriander seeds

½ teaspoon turmeric powder

½ teaspoon cayenne pepper

½ teaspoon yellow
mustard seeds

½ teaspoon sea salt

2 bay leaves

¼ cup fresh cilantro (optional)

2 tablespoons cashews

1 tablespoon shredded coconut

1 tablespoon coconut oil

1 tablespoon tomato paste

INSTRUCTIONS

1. In a small saucepan, combine the garlic, ginger, paprika, garam masala, cumin, coriander, turmeric, cayenne, mustard seeds, salt, and bay leaves. Toast over medium heat, stirring occasionally so nothing burns, until the mixture becomes fragrant, 4 to 5 minutes.
2. Transfer the spice blend to a spice grinder or blender and pulse into a fine powder. Pour into a small bowl.
3. In a spice grinder or blender, combine the cilantro, cashews, and shredded coconut and pulse into a fine, green powder.
4. In the small bowl with the toasted spice blend, add cilantro mixture, coconut oil, and tomato paste. Stir until well combined. Transfer to a small airtight container and store in the fridge for 7 to 10 days.

Thai Green Curry Paste

• •

MAKES ABOUT 1 CUP

This bright curry paste is surprisingly easy to make, and so much healthier and fresher-tasting than the store-bought variety. The most essential component is, of course, the Thai green chiles, which give it color and heat. The rest is pretty simple: tamari for something salty, lemongrass and cilantro for some aromatics, as well as shallots and garlic, which give the curry pungency and depth. This paste makes enough for one large pot of curry to serve 3 or 4 hungry people (see page 178), but feel free to make a double batch of the paste and freeze half for later.

INGREDIENTS

1 teaspoon coriander seeds

1 teaspoon cumin seeds

½ teaspoon ground white pepper

5 or 6 Thai green chiles, stemmed and chopped

3 cloves garlic, chopped

2 shallots, chopped

2 stalks fresh lemongrass, outer leaves removed and chopped

1 (1-inch) piece fresh ginger, peeled and chopped

1 cup lightly packed chopped fresh cilantro

½ cup chopped green bell pepper

1 tablespoon tamari

Zest and juice of 1 lime

½ teaspoon sea salt

INSTRUCTIONS

1. In a small skillet, toast the coriander and cumin seeds over medium heat for about 2 minutes, or until fragrant. Transfer to a spice grinder and grind into a fine powder.
2. In a food processor, combine the ground spices with the remaining ingredients and process for 2 to 3 minutes, until the mixture becomes a smooth, thick paste. Occasionally stop to scrape down the sides of the processor bowl. If needed, add a tablespoon or two of water to get the mixture moving. Store the paste in an airtight container in the fridge for up to 1 week.

Curry

· · · · · · · · ·

SERVES 3 TO 4

INGREDIENTS

1 recipe Thai Green Curry
Paste (page 176)

1 (13.5-ounce) can full-
fat coconut milk

Cubed tofu and chopped
vegetables of your choice

Cooked rice, for serving

INSTRUCTIONS

1. In a large saucepan, heat the curry paste over
   medium heat for about 2 minutes.
2. Stir in the coconut milk and 1 cup water, plus
   the tofu and any chopped vegetables you desire.
   Simmer until the vegetables are tender. Serve
   with rice.

Gluten-Free Flour Mix

. . . .

MAKES 6½ CUPS

When I first started baking without gluten, I remember how overwhelmed I felt about all the different flours available. Unlike baking with wheat, where all you really need is all-purpose flour, baking without gluten requires a mix of different flours and starches to create the right texture and flavor. The store-bought mixes are terribly expensive, and my goodness, are those packages small. So I started making my own. This particular blend is a great substitute in recipes that call for regular flour, and it is used in many of the recipes in this book. Keep a batch on hand for all your gluten-free baking needs. —N. A.

INGREDIENTS

3 cups chickpea flour

2 cups brown rice flour

1 cup potato starch
(not potato flour)

½ cup tapioca starch

INSTRUCTIONS

Combine all the ingredients in a large bowl and whisk thoroughly to combine. Store in an airtight container in a cool, dry place for up to 12 months.

Homestyle Banana-Walnut Muffin Mix

MAKES ENOUGH MIX FOR 12 MUFFINS

What's not to love about a homemade banana muffin? We sure can't tell you. Brimming with ripe 'nanas, loaded with whole grains and nuts, and gently sweetened with coconut sugar, these soft and wholesome breakfast buddies are sure to give you a solid start to the day. Use this mix for the Banana-Walnut Muffins on page 181. Try slathering on some homemade almond butter (see page 106) for a little extra pep in your step.

INGREDIENTS

1 cup oat flour

⅔ cup buckwheat flour

½ cup almond meal

½ cup coconut sugar

2 teaspoons baking powder

1 teaspoon ground cinnamon

½ teaspoon baking soda

¼ teaspoon sea salt

⅛ teaspoon freshly grated nutmeg

⅓ cup chopped walnuts

INSTRUCTIONS

In a large bowl, whisk together all the ingredients except the walnuts. Stir in the walnuts. Store in an airtight container at room temperature for up to 6 months.

Banana-Walnut Muffins

. . . .

MAKES 12 MUFFINS

INGREDIENTS

1½ cups pureed banana
(from about 3 overripe
medium bananas)

¾ cup unsweetened
nondairy milk

1 recipe Homestyle
Banana-Walnut Muffin Mix
(opposite)

TIP: The easiest way
to puree bananas is in
a deep cup using an
immersion blender,
then measure out 1½
cups of the puree.

INSTRUCTIONS

1. Preheat the oven to 350°F.
   Line a 12-cup muffin tin with
   paper liners.
2. In a large bowl, stir together
   the pureed banana and
   nondairy milk until smooth.
   Add the muffin mix and stir to combine.
3. Divide the batter evenly among the wells of the
   prepared pan. Bake for 18 to 20 minutes, or until
   a toothpick inserted into the center of a muffin
   comes out clean. Remove from the oven and
   let cool for 10 minutes before transferring to a
   cooling rack. Store in an airtight container in the
   fridge for up to 3 days or in the freezer for 2 to 3
   months.

. . . .

Freeze overripe bananas!
A good way to preserve an
overload of overripe bananas
is to peel, chop, and freeze
them for later use in baking
or smoothie-making (or to
make Fruity Soft Serve, page
61). Simply defrost and mash
them with a fork in a large
bowl for use in this recipe.

. . . .

Chocolate Cake Mix (opposite) and
Creamy Peanut Butter Frosting (page 210)

Chocolate Cake Mix

MAKES ENOUGH MIX FOR ONE 9-INCH CAKE OR 12 CUPCAKES

We made so many cakes in your honor. Knowing this recipe could become your go-to for every birthday, dinner party, and soiree, we knew it had to be perfect. After all the testing and tasting, we are proud to proclaim this is one extraordinary cake mix. The crumb is moist and fluffy, and the flavor is deep chocolate decadence. Since you never know when you'll have an excuse to party, we suggest you always keep a batch on hand. Use this mix for Chocolate Cake on page 184. It pairs beautifully with Creamy Peanut Butter Frosting (page 210) and Chocolate Fudge Frosting (page 209).

INGREDIENTS

1½ cups unbleached all-purpose flour

½ cup cocoa powder

6 tablespoons coconut sugar

1 teaspoon baking soda

½ teaspoon sea salt

½ teaspoon ground cinnamon

INSTRUCTIONS

In a medium bowl, whisk together all the ingredients. Store in an airtight container at room temperature for up to 6 months.

MAKE IT GLUTEN-FREE:
Replace the all-purpose flour with an equal amount of Gluten-Free Flour Mix (page 179), add 1 cup fine almond flour, ½ teaspoon xanthan gum, and an extra ½ cup cocoa powder.

Chocolate Cake

INGREDIENTS

1 recipe Chocolate Cake Mix

½ cup coffee or water

½ cup almond or soy milk (vanilla flavor preferred)

½ cup canola oil

½ cup pure maple syrup

2 tablespoons apple cider vinegar

> **TIP:** If you don't have a vanilla-flavored nondairy milk, just add ½ teaspoon pure vanilla extract.

INSTRUCTIONS

1. Preheat the oven to 350°F. Lightly grease a 9-inch cake pan with coconut oil or line a 12-cup muffin tin with paper liners.
2. In a large bowl, sift the dry cake mix ingredients using a fine-mesh sieve.
3. In a medium bowl, mix together the coffee, almond milk, oil, maple syrup, and vinegar.
4. Add the liquid ingredients to the bowl with the cake mix and whisk gently until there are no large clumps remaining.
5. Pour the batter into the prepared pan. Bake for 22 to 27 minutes in the cake pan or 20 to 25 minutes in the muffin tin. The cake/cupcakes can be stored in an airtight container in the fridge for up to 5 days or frozen for 2 to 3 months.

> **MAKE IT GLUTEN-FREE:** Use the Gluten-Free Chocolate Cake Mix option (page 183) and add an additional ½ cup almond milk to the wet ingredients in the batter. Due to the extra volume, the gluten-free cake works best when divided between two 9-inch pans or 18 muffin cups for baking.

Easy-Bake Oatmeal-Raisin Cookie Mix

. . . .

MAKES ENOUGH MIX FOR 12 TO 14 COOKIES

You'll love the comforting, traditional taste of these chewy, raisin-studded cookies. We don't how oats and raisins first came together but we think they have become true best friends in this mix. Use it to make the Oatmeal-Raisin Cookies on page 186. If you're feeling adventurous, throw in a handful of chocolate chips or walnuts instead, then bake them up and dunk one in a cold glass of nondairy milk. You deserve it.

INGREDIENTS

1¼ cups spelt or whole wheat flour

¾ cup rolled oats

⅔ cup coconut sugar

½ cup almond meal

2 tablespoons flax meal

½ teaspoon baking soda

½ teaspoon ground cinnamon

¼ teaspoon vanilla powder, or 1 vanilla bean, halved lengthwise and seeds scraped

¼ teaspoon sea salt

½ cup raisins

INSTRUCTIONS

In a large bowl, whisk together all the ingredients except the raisins. Stir in the raisins. Store in an airtight container at room temperature for up to 6 months.

> **MAKE IT GLUTEN-FREE:**
> Replace the spelt flour with an equal amount of Gluten-Free Flour Mix (page 179).

Oatmeal-Raisin Cookies

. . . .

MAKES 12 TO 14 COOKIES

INGREDIENTS

⅓ cup coconut oil

¼ cup nondairy milk

1 recipe Easy-Bake Oatmeal-Raisin Cookie Mix (page 185)

INSTRUCTIONS

1. Preheat the oven to 375°F. Line a baking sheet with parchment paper.
2. In a small saucepan, melt the coconut oil over medium-low heat. Whisk in the nondairy milk. Remove from the heat and pour into a large bowl. Add the cookie mix and stir until the dough comes together.
3. Form balls of about 2 tablespoons of dough each and place on the prepared cookie pan about 2 to 3 inches apart. Use the bottom of a glass to gently flatten each ball.
4. Bake for 10 to 12 minutes, until golden brown. Remove from the oven and let cool completely (they are quite soft right out of the oven). Store in a cookie tin at room temperature for up to 5 days or in the freezer for 2 to 3 months.

Peppermint Hot Chocolate

. . . .

SERVES 1

INGREDIENTS

1 cup nondairy milk

1 to 2 Peppermint Patty Hot Chocolate Pucks (opposite)

INSTRUCTIONS

Bring the nondairy milk to a slow simmer over low heat. Add the hot chocolate pucks and let stand for 5 minutes. Stir the mixture until all of the chocolate has dissolved. Serve immediately.

Peppermint Patty Hot Chocolate Pucks

MAKES 8 PUCKS

Memories are made over steaming cups of cocoa. These single-serving peppermint hot chocolate portions are ideal for stuffing into stockings, tying onto parcels and packages, or dropping off as housewarming gifts to friends and neighbors. These keep well in the freezer for months, making them an ideal make-ahead treat to get you through those cold winter nights. Use the pucks to make the Peppermint Hot Chocolate on page 186.

INGREDIENTS

3.5 ounces 71% cocoa dairy-free dark chocolate

¼ cup cocoa powder

¼ cup pure maple syrup, at room temperature

1 tablespoon pure peppermint extract

¼ cup vanilla sugar (page 193), or ¼ cup cane sugar infused with a vanilla bean

Pinch of sea salt

INSTRUCTIONS

1. Melt the chocolate using a double boiler (see instructions on page 32).
2. In a small bowl, combine the cocoa powder, maple syrup, peppermint extract, vanilla sugar, and salt.
3. Add the melted chocolate and stir until well mixed. The mixture will firm, but don't worry, it will still melt smoothly.
4. Divide the mixture evenly among eight small chocolate molds or ice cube molds. Refrigerate until firm. Once firm, transfer to an airtight container and store in the fridge or freezer for up to 3 months.

TIP: The vanilla sugar needs to be made in a spice grinder, or little bits of vanilla bean will remain and impact the texture of your hot chocolate. If you don't have a spice grinder, replace the vanilla sugar by adding a split vanilla bean to your cane sugar and allowing it to infuse for a few days.

Cookie Dough (page 220)

CHAPTER 7

Sweet Treats Made Real

· ·

WE ALWAYS SAY THAT COOKING done with care is an act of love. Putting in a little effort to make something sweet to share feeds our souls and nurtures our relationships. The good news is that making many standard desserts truly homemade is easier than ever, and more satisfying than thawing a frozen, beige pound cake on your kitchen counter.

In this chapter, you'll find tips and techniques for making fresh flour from whole grains; piping perfect white chocolate chips; preparing premade pie crusts; and creating all your own make-ahead favorites like frozen cookie dough and ice cream sandwiches. We're offering a colossal cornucopia of confections you'd be proud to share at every one of life's celebrations. These recipes are as simple as they are useful—plus, with gluten-free alternatives for each treat, we've got you all covered. It's pie o'clock—let's bake.

Basic Fresh Flours

YIELD VARIES

Making our own fresh flours was truly the first step in our DIY journey. We were moving away from more processed ingredients and were looking for nutrient-dense alternatives. The terms nut flour and nut meal are used interchangeably, but in practice, nut flours, particularly those made with almonds, are often made from blanched (skins-removed) nuts to produce a lighter texture, and nut meal is made from whole, raw nuts (with the skin intact). We prefer the latter, but for most recipes you can use flour or meal and get good results either way.

Some of our favorite flours to use in baking, cereals, and raw desserts include almond, oat, cashew, hazelnut, coconut, buckwheat, and millet. These pantry staples are superstars, incredibly versatile and incredibly delicious. Take almonds as an example—you can use them to make a creamy milk, grind into thick, spreadable butter, blend into flour for pancakes, or save the pulp for Almond Pulp Cookie Crumbs (page 223). Amazing! No need to buy each of those products (milk, butter, flour) separately when you can just invest in a great big bag of almonds and make what you need, when you need it. Many of the recipes in this book call for fresh flours to provide a healthful base for baked goods that is also gluten- and grain-free.

Flours made in a blender are slightly finer than those made in a food processor, but not to worry, both will work well in most recipes (including all the ones in this book).

INGREDIENTS

At least ⅓ cup nuts (almonds, cashews, hazelnuts, etc.), shredded coconut, rolled oats, raw buckwheat groats, or uncooked millet grains

INSTRUCTIONS

In a blender or food processor, pulse the base (nuts, coconut, oats, groats, or grains), scraping down the sides as needed, until a fine flour forms. Fresh flours are best used within a couple of days. During that time, they will keep well in the fridge. To extend their freshness to weeks or months, store them in the freezer in an airtight container or sandwich bag.

TIPS: *In a blender:* As a blender has a powerful motor, we recommend starting a nut flour at low speed for a couple of seconds before turning it up to high to turn the nuts into a fine meal. Scrape down the sides and pulse rather than letting the blender run. This will keep the blender from heating up and causing the nuts to turn into a paste. It should only take 30 to 45 seconds to turn almonds or cashews into a flour. With dry grains or coconut, you can simply turn the blender to a high speed, stopping to scrape down the sides every few seconds, and blend until it becomes a fine meal.

In a food processor: A food processor is a great alternative to a blender when you're making a big batch of flour. If you're only making a little, sometimes it is hard for the food processor blades to catch all of the little bits of the grains (so just make a little more and save it for later). As with the blender, we suggest using the pulse button and stopping to scrape down the sides when making a flour out of nuts to avoid making a paste or nut butter instead. It should take less than a minute to create a flour from nuts. Grains become a flour much faster, and because of their lower fat content, you can leave the food processor running for the 20 to 30 seconds it will take to create a fine flour.

Vanilla Extract

. . . .

MAKES 1 CUP

Vanilla is intoxicating and exotic. But the world's love for this unbelievable bean has made it so ubiquitous in recipes that the word vanilla has been redefined as boring or plain. Well, we believe using fresh vanilla beans, powders, and extracts make your results anything but. Since a teaspoon of vanilla extract can elevate an entire dish, we like to make sure we always have a supply (those extract bottles are just so tiny), so we make our own—in big batches. Homemade vanilla extract makes a wonderful gift for your fellow baking fiends. We suggest using the best vodka and the freshest vanilla beans you can find. Using the best ingredients to create your extract will infuse all your future treats with extra deliciousness.

Unlike most recipes in this book, this one takes some forward thinking—five months, in fact—but since it only takes a couple of minutes to prep, this could become a monthly routine that pays off in huge, delicious dividends. Don't forget to label your jars with a date so you know when your extract is ready to use.

INGREDIENTS

1 cup vodka

3 plump, soft vanilla beans

TIP: If you have a dish-washer, you can sanitize your jar by running a rinse wash at a high temperature setting. If you don't have a dishwasher, wash the jar, then pour in some boiling water and let stand for a couple of seconds before pouring it out and adding the vodka.

INSTRUCTIONS

1. Pour the vodka into a very clean glass jar with a lid.
2. Using a small knife, slit each of the vanilla beans in half lengthwise.
3. Add the vanilla beans to the jar of vodka. Close the lid tightly. Place the jar in a cool, dark place and let the vanilla infuse the vodka for at least 5 months.

TRY THIS: Vanilla extract can also be made with bourbon rather than vodka.

Lavender Sugar

· · · · · · · · · · · · · · · · · · · ·

MAKES ¼ CUP

This is an amazing addition to lemonade, Popsicles, ice creams, jams, and cookies. If you don't like pieces of lavender in the finished product, just strain it out once the flavor is infused.

INGREDIENTS

¼ cup cane sugar

1 tablespoon dried culinary lavender

INSTRUCTIONS

In a spice grinder, combine the sugar and lavender and pulse to blend. Store in an airtight container at room temperature for up to 6 months.

Vanilla Sugar

· · · · · · · · · · · · · · · · · ·

MAKES ½ CUP

This incredible infused sugar is fantastic to add to your favorite baked goods, stir into coffee, or sprinkle on cookies.

INGREDIENTS

¼ cup coarsely chopped vanilla bean pods, hard ends removed before chopping

¼ cup cane sugar

INSTRUCTIONS

In a spice grinder, combine the vanilla bean pods and sugar and grind until well combined. Store in an airtight container at room temperature for up to 6 months.

Quick Caramel Sauce

Intimidated by the thought of making your own caramel? Don't be. It can all happen right on your stovetop without sugar or butter or cooking thermometers. The process is simple, and within just a few minutes, you'll have an incredible sweet sauce that can be drizzled over ice cream sundaes or cake slices, or used as a dip for pretzels or chocolate. Seriously, it's all you could ever want from a caramel sauce!

INGREDIENTS

½ cup brown rice syrup

¼ cup pure maple syrup

2 tablespoons macadamia or cashew butter, or a combination (page 106)

¼ teaspoon sea salt

2 tablespoons nondairy milk or water

1 teaspoon pure vanilla extract

INSTRUCTIONS

1. Combine the brown rice syrup, maple syrup, macadamia butter, and salt in a small saucepan. Bring to a boil over medium heat.

2. Reduce the heat to low and simmer for about 5 minutes, or until the liquid is thick enough to coat the back of a spoon. Remove from the heat and whisk in the nondairy milk and vanilla. The caramel can be stored in a mason jar in the fridge for about 2 months. It will thicken once refrigerated, giving it the perfect consistency for drizzling over ice cream or other desserts.

Simple Chocolate Syrup

· ·

MAKES ¾ CUP

This homemade syrup is a super-simple way to get your chocolate fix. Our tester Cintia quickly became addicted as she drizzled it over bowls of fruit and banana soft serve each night until it was all gone. We also use it to make delicious chocolate milk with Basic Nut/Seed Milk (page 37) or chocolate swirl ice cream using the Vanilla Bean Ice Cream on page 62. The options are endless.

INGREDIENTS

⅓ cup pure maple syrup

¼ cup cocoa powder

1 tablespoon coconut oil

Pinch of sea salt

½ teaspoon pure
vanilla extract

INSTRUCTIONS

1. In a small saucepan, whisk together the maple syrup, cocoa powder, coconut oil, salt, and 2 tablespoons water. Cook over medium heat, whisking slowly, until the coconut oil has melted and the mixture is smooth and shiny.
2. Remove from the heat and stir in the vanilla. The syrup can be stored in a mason jar in the fridge for up to 1 month. It will thicken once refrigerated.

Date Paste

· ·

MAKES 1½ CUPS

Date paste is a fairly standard ingredient in raw dessert recipes and is one of our preferred ways to sweeten raw desserts. It involves an extra step beyond using agave or maple syrup, but it is well worth it. Date paste can be made ahead and stored in the refrigerator for a couple of weeks. Even if you're keeping things simple, date paste is a great addition to smoothies, a nut butter sandwich, or just a sliced apple.

INGREDIENTS

1½ cups Medjool dates, pitted and soaked in water until soft (about 30 minutes)

INSTRUCTIONS

1. Drain the soaked dates.
2. In a blender, blend the dates and as much water as is needed to achieve a smooth, thick paste (about ½ cup). You may need to stop and scrape down the sides of the blender container a few times along the way. Store the paste in an airtight container in the fridge for up to 1 month.

Lemon Curd

MAKES 2 CUPS

This light and refreshing lemon curd is reminiscent of the incredible lemon meringue pie my grandma Martin used to make during my childhood—for family dinners, bake sales, or just about anytime someone requested it. This vegan spin on my grandma's classic might be better than the old favorite. It's a pie filling, spread, and dessert topping all in one, and oh so good. Share this lemony pleasure at your next party and your guests will be begging for more. —N. A.

INGREDIENTS

1¾ cups unsweetened almond milk

½ cup pure maple syrup

3 tablespoons agar flakes, or 2 teaspoons agar powder

1 tablespoon fresh lemon zest

¾ cup fresh lemon juice (from about 3 lemons)

2 tablespoons tapioca flour

⅛ teaspoon turmeric powder

Pinch of sea salt

1 teaspoon pure vanilla extract

INSTRUCTIONS

1. In a medium saucepan, combine the almond milk, maple syrup, and agar. Whisk vigorously until no clumps of agar remain. Bring to a boil over medium heat. Reduce the heat to low and simmer, whisking occasionally, for 10 minutes.
2. While the agar mixture is simmering, combine the lemon zest, lemon juice, tapioca flour, turmeric, and salt in a small bowl and whisk until the tapioca has dissolved.
3. After 10 minutes, add the lemon mixture to the saucepan and raise the heat to medium. Whisk continuously as the mixture thickens.
4. When bubbles start to form on the surface, continue whisking for 30 seconds more. Remove from the heat and stir in the vanilla.
5. Pour the lemon curd into a shallow bowl and let cool to room temperature. Refrigerate for about 2 hours, until firm.
6. Transfer the curd to a blender and blend until smooth. The curd can be stored in a mason jar in the fridge for up to 2 weeks.

Vanilla Cream

MAKES 3 CUPS

This is vegan decadence at its best. If you're a sucker for anything luxurious and vanilla flavored, this stuff is a must. Once it's blended, it can be poured over just about anything, but if you want a thicker, scoopable cream, allow it to sit in the fridge overnight. Use it to layer in granola or fruit parfaits, or serve with French toast or special occasion desserts.

INGREDIENTS

1 cup raw cashews, soaked in water for 6 hours

1 (13.5-ounce) can full-fat coconut milk

¼ cup pure maple syrup

1 teaspoon fresh lemon juice

¼ teaspoon vanilla powder, or 1 vanilla bean, halved lengthwise and seeds scraped

Pinch of sea salt

TIP: Soak the cashews ahead of time and store in the fridge for up to 2 days.

INSTRUCTIONS

1. Drain and rinse the cashews.
2. In a blender, combine all the ingredients and blend until very smooth. Stop and scrape down the sides of the blender container as needed. Use immediately or store in a mason jar in the fridge up to 12 days. The cream should thicken to a scoopable consistency once refrigerated overnight.

Chocolate Pudding Snack Packs

SERVES 3 TO 4

We don't know anyone who would turn away an offer of chocolate pudding. This perfectly rich, easy-to-make treat far surpasses those handy lunch box pudding cups and is just as convenient. Throw a few ingredients into a blender and then divide the pudding among mini mason jars for a ridiculously charming little treat that will make you feel like a kid again.

INGREDIENTS

1 (13.5-ounce) can full-fat coconut milk

⅓ cup pure maple syrup

¼ cup cocoa powder

2 tablespoons chia seeds

1 teaspoon pure vanilla extract

¼ teaspoon sea salt

1½ ounces dairy-free chocolate, chopped, or ¼ cup chocolate chips

INSTRUCTIONS

1. In a blender, combine the coconut milk, maple syrup, cocoa powder, chia seeds, vanilla, and salt and blend until the chia seeds are fully pulverized and the mixture is smooth.
2. Melt the chocolate using a double boiler (see instructions on page 32) and add to the mixture in the blender. Blend to combine.
3. Transfer the pudding to a shallow bowl and refrigerate until it is cold and thick, ideally 3 hours or more. Divide among small mason jars for a convenient to-go treat. Store in the fridge for up to 1 week.

Almond Press-In Pie Crust (no-bake option)

MAKES 1 SINGLE PIE OR TART CRUST

Once you've whipped up this simple raw crust, you can make anything from a large pie or mini tarts to a decadent raw cheesecake. Pair it with the Classic Vanilla Cheesecake filling on page 200, the Chocolate Fudge Filling on page 209, or even the Lemon Curd on page 196.

INGREDIENTS

1½ cups raw almonds

½ cup unsweetened shredded coconut

¾ cup pitted Medjool dates (see tip)

1½ tablespoons melted coconut oil

½ teaspoon pure vanilla extract

Pinch of sea salt

TIP: It's best to use soft dates, as they help the ingredients hold together. If yours have hardened somewhat, just soak them in a bowl of warm water for 10 minutes and drain well before using.

INSTRUCTIONS

1. In a food processor, combine the almonds and shredded coconut and process to a fine meal (take care not to overprocess, or it will turn into a paste).
2. Add the dates and process to fully combine.
3. Add the coconut oil, vanilla, and salt and process until a dough comes together. The dough should stick together when pressed between your thumb and forefinger. If it seems dry, add water, 1 teaspoon at a time, and process again.
4. Press the dough into a 9-inch pie plate, springform pan, or tart pan with a removable bottom. Use your fingers to evenly distribute and press the dough around the base and up the sides of the plate or pan (if using a springform pan to make a raw cheesecake, you can just press it evenly over the bottom). Place in the freezer to firm up before filling. The crust can be frozen for up to 1 month if wrapped tightly in plastic wrap and then aluminum foil.

Have you ever admired those beautifully swirled cheesecakes at your local café? It is far easier than you'd imagine to pull off. You just need a bit of confidence, as being too timid with your pour can make the accent flavor pool on top of your cheesecake rather than getting mixed into dramatic swirls. Simply reserve a cup of the filling mixture and blend with the flavor addition of your choice (berry, chocolate, caramel, lavender). Transfer to a spouted measuring cup. Here's the tough part: slowly but consistently pour the mixture in a number of spots around the top of your cheesecake (forceful pours of about 1 tablespoon or so spread out across the cheesecake); you want to actually break the surface of the cheesecake with each pour. Then take a knife and swirl out from each of the spots where you added the accent flavor, in a circular motion. Do a little and take stock. You don't want the swirls to overtake the cake; you'd like it to look like a wonderful added bonus.

Classic Vanilla Cheesecake

MAKES ONE 10-INCH CHEESECAKE

Raw vegan desserts have been all the rage in recent days. Some of them are decadent confections that highlight the undeniable richness of ingredients like cashews and coconut—a richness that many believed was impossible to achieve without dairy. It seems like some kind of alchemy that such a heavenly dessert can be created with plants. One bite of this pie and you'll start to believe in magic.

This classic raw cheesecake is easy to pull together and doesn't require the water bath or oven time that a more traditional pie would. However, it is a bit temperamental in warm temperatures, so keep it cool and firm in the freezer until you're ready to serve.

INGREDIENTS

1 cup raw cashews, soaked in water for 6 hours

1¼ cups unsweetened almond milk

1 cup pure maple syrup

¼ cup fresh lemon juice

2 vanilla bean pods, halved lengthwise and seeds scraped

½ teaspoon sea salt

½ cup coconut oil, melted

¼ cup cacao butter, melted

1 recipe Almond Press-In Pie Crust (page 199)

INSTRUCTIONS

1. In a blender, combine the cashews, almond milk, maple syrup, lemon juice, vanilla bean seeds, and salt. Blend until completely smooth.

2. Add the coconut oil and cacao butter and pulse until well incorporated. Be careful not to overmix at this point, as the fat can separate if exposed to the heat from the blender motor for too long.

3. Pour the mixture into the prepared crust and freeze until firm. Fully prepared cheesecake can be wrapped and frozen for 1 month. Serve directly from the freezer, letting the cheesecake soften just enough to slice, 10 to 15 minutes, depending on the season.

TRY THIS: This is a great basic cheesecake filling that can easily be transformed into a myriad of variations with a few simple additions. You can top it with the Oh My Cherry Pie Filling (page 205) for a classic New York cheesecake slice, or try adding raspberries, strawberries, blueberries, lavender, chocolate sauce, or caramel sauce when blending to create something fun and flavorful to impress your guests.

Premade Pie Crust

· ·

MAKES 1 SINGLE CRUST

This flaky, buttery, all-purpose pie crust is easy as can be using your food processor. No need to freeze all your bowls, spoons, and ingredients beforehand—the only secret (that isn't really a secret) is to freeze the whole pan before baking to prevent shrinkage and the need for pie weights. While you're at it, make another that you can have on hand for all your pie crust needs. This crust suits just about any pie filling but is especially good paired with Pumpkin Pie filling (page 207), the Oh My Cherry Pie Filling (page 205), or the Lemon Curd (page 196).

INGREDIENTS

1 cup whole wheat pastry flour

¾ cup unbleached all-purpose flour

1 tablespoon coconut sugar or cane sugar

¼ teaspoon sea salt

½ cup plus 1 tablespoon solid coconut oil (see tip, page 86)

1 teaspoon pure vanilla extract

½ tablespoon apple cider vinegar

MAKE IT GLUTEN-FREE:
Replace the whole wheat pastry flour and unbleached all-purpose flour with 1¾ cups Gluten-Free Flour Mix (page 179).

INSTRUCTIONS

1. In a food processor, combine the pastry flour, all-purpose flour, coconut sugar, and salt and pulse until combined.
2. Add the coconut oil and process until thoroughly combined and there are no chunks of coconut oil remaining. Add 3 tablespoons water, the vanilla, and the vinegar and process until the dough comes together and starts to form a ball on the blade. If needed, add more water, 1 teaspoon at a time, and process again until the dough comes together.
3. Place the dough on a large piece of parchment paper and shape it into a disc with your hands. Place another piece of parchment paper of equal size on top and use a rolling pin to roll from the center out. As you roll out the dough, rotate the paper so you roll in different directions to produce an even 11-inch circle, about ⅛ inch thick (see page 26 for tips). Remove the top piece of parchment paper.
4. Have a 9-inch pie plate or tart pan ready to go. Working quickly, slip your hand under the bottom parchment paper to lift up the dough and gently flip it into the plate. Remove the parchment paper and use your fingertips to

Premade Pie Crust (opposite),
Chocolate Fudge Frosting or
Filling (page 209)

press the dough evenly and gently into the pan while rotating the pan every so often. If using a pie plate, flute or crimp the edges of the dough.

5. Pierce the dough with a fork to prevent air pockets from forming when baking, and freeze it, uncovered, for about 30 minutes. If storing for a longer period, wrap tightly in plastic wrap and then aluminum foil, and freeze for up to 1 month (transfer to the fridge to thaw for 15 minutes before baking).

6. At this point, follow your recipe instructions on how to fill and bake the crust. If a fully baked crust is needed, bake at 350°F for 30 minutes, or until golden. Let cool before filling.

Oh My Cherry Pie Filling

· ·

MAKES ABOUT 2 CUPS

You may have seen that red, glossy, gloppy canned cherry pie filling spread on top of cakes and tarts. Well, as ardent cherry lovers, we just had to create a version that truly let the cherries and not the sweet goop be the star. Although called a pie filling, this recipe also offers a solution for all of your decadent garnishing dilemmas (you have those, right?). You can make a show-stopping treat by topping the Classic Vanilla Cheesecake (page 200) and topping it with a generous layer of cherry pie filling. Just allow the cheesecake filling to firm up completely before topping with the cherries—garnish with a few curls of chocolate and you'll get a gold star for sure. Or bake a cake using the Chocolate Cake Mix (page 183); once cooled, cut the cake in half horizontally, spread the bottom layer with about half the cherry pie filling, then carefully place the top layer on top. Coat the whole big beautiful cake with frosting and serve with some Vanilla Bean Ice Cream (page 62). Or, of course, you could make a pie (recipe follows).

INGREDIENTS

2 tablespoons pure
maple syrup

1 tablespoon fresh lemon juice

2½ teaspoons arrowroot
powder

Pinch of sea salt

2 cups sweet cherries,
pitted (thawed, if frozen)

½ teaspoon pure
vanilla extract

INSTRUCTIONS

1. In a small saucepan over medium heat, whisk together the maple syrup, lemon juice, arrowroot powder, salt, and ¼ cup water until well combined and the arrowroot has completely dissolved.
2. Add the cherries and cook for 3 to 5 minutes, until the liquid begins to thicken and become a deep purple color. Remove from the heat and stir in the vanilla.
3. Transfer to a heatproof container with a lid and chill in the fridge. It will become much thicker as it cools. Store in the fridge for up to 7 days.

Cherry Pie

· · · · · · · · · · · · · · · ·

MAKES 1 PIE

INGREDIENTS

2 Premade Pie Crusts
(page 202), unbaked

3 Oh My Cherry Pie Fillings
(page 205), cooled 30
minutes or made up to
1 week in advance.

INSTRUCTIONS

1. Preheat the oven to 425°F.
2. Roll out half of the Premade Pie Crust dough and press into a 9-inch pie pan (see instructions on page 202).
3. Pour the cooled Oh My Cherry Pie Filling into the pie crust and spread out evenly.
4. Roll out the top pie crust dough between two pieces of parchment paper until the dough is ¼ to ⅛ inch thick. Using a pizza cutter or a sharp knife, gently cut the crust into long strips, about 1 inch wide.
5. Create a lattice pattern over the pie by placing the strips in one direction over the pie, leaving 1 to 2 inches of space between each strip.
6. Fold back every other strip of crust until only 1 inch of the strip is over the pie filling. Then place a strip of crust across the pie, sliding it right up to where the folded-back strips touch the pie (it should be perpendicular to the strips of crust already on the pie).
7. Unfold the folded strips back across the pie. Continue to weave the crust by repeating the process above, alternating the folded and unfolded strips of crust each time you add the perpendicular piece.
8. Reduce the oven temperature to 350°F. Place the pie on a baking sheet and slide it into the oven. Bake for 30 to 35 minutes until the cherry filling begins to bubble and the crust is lightly browned.
9. Let cool for at least 40 minutes before slicing. Serve with a scoop of Vanilla Bean Ice Cream (page 62).

Pumpkin Pie

. . . .

MAKES ONE 9-INCH PIE

This fall-themed pie filling favorite is creamy, spicy, and not too sweet. Paired with the Premade Pie Crust, it makes a perfect vegan pumpkin pie. See the sidebar if you've got time for freshly roasted fall pumpkin; otherwise, canned pumpkin puree will do just fine.

INGREDIENTS

FILLING

2 cups pumpkin puree (see sidebar)

1 cup full-fat coconut milk

¼ cup pure maple syrup

¼ cup coconut sugar

¼ cup oat flour

1 tablespoon Pumpkin Pie Spice (page 170)

¼ teaspoon sea salt

1 teaspoon pure vanilla extract

CRUST

1 recipe Premade Pie Crust (page 202), unbaked

INSTRUCTIONS

1. In a blender, combine all the filling ingredients and blend until very smooth, scraping down the sides of the blender container as needed. (At this point, the filling can be stored in an airtight container in the fridge for up to 3 days.)
2. Preheat the oven to 425°F.
3. Pour the filling into the prepared crust, using a spatula to distribute the filling evenly and smooth out the top. Bake the pie for 10 minutes, then reduce the oven temperature to 350°F and bake for 30 minutes more, until the crust is golden and the filling has mostly set (the center may be soft, but it will set further as it cools).
4. Remove from the oven and transfer to a cooling rack. Let cool completely, then transfer to the fridge to chill and set. For best results, refrigerate overnight.

. . . .

PUMPKIN PUREE—CANNED VS. HOMEMADE

We tend to agree that fresh is always best, but there are a few reasons why canned pumpkin puree is so popular: it is convenient, relatively inexpensive, and it means pumpkin pie all year round. Most important, though, it is consistent. Canned pumpkin puree does not vary much in thickness, texture, or flavor.

Homemade pumpkin puree can be just as good as canned, but it takes some prep work. If you are using fresh pumpkin, do not use the jack-o'-lantern type; the flesh of these large pumpkins is too watery and stringy. Instead, look for small pumpkins, often called sugar pie pumpkins. To bake, cut 2 pie pumpkins in half and remove the seeds and stringy bits. Set the pumpkin halves, cut side down, in a baking pan. Bake at 400°F for 30 to 40 minutes, until soft. Let cool, then scoop out the cooked flesh and puree in a food processor.

. . . .

Premade Pie Crust (page 202), Chocolate Fudge Frosting or Filling (opposite), and Whipped Cream (page 40)

Chocolate Fudge Frosting or Filling

MAKES 2 CUPS

An ongoing project in our kitchens is creating a luscious chocolate frosting that can rival the traditional margarine-shortening-sugar concoction. We tried a number of alternatives, but this version won us over as soon as the first spoonful touched our lips. Good quality dark chocolate combined with a little coconut milk and avocado give this frosting a smooth, rich texture that makes it irresistible. It's great for piping into swirly mountains on cupcakes, spreading into a thick layer atop a cake, or even poured directly into a pie shell for an elegant yet easy dinner party dessert.

HOW TO MAKE A SIMPLE CHOCOLATE TART

Want an easy, chocolaty, showstopping dessert? Because this filling is more rich than over-the-top sweet, it also makes an incredible filling for a pie or tart (use the Premade Pie Crust on page 202 or the Almond Press-In Pie Crust on page 199). After step 2, simply pour the mixture into the premade crust and freeze until firm, about 1 hour. Serve with Whipped Cream (page 40) and fresh berries.

INGREDIENTS

7 ounces 70% cocoa dairy-free dark chocolate, finely chopped

½ cup full-fat coconut milk

2 tablespoons coconut oil

½ cup pureed avocado (see tip)

¼ cup pure maple syrup

2 teaspoons pure vanilla extract

Pinch of sea salt

Nondairy milk (if needed)

INSTRUCTIONS

1. Melt the chocolate, coconut milk, and coconut oil in a double boiler (see instructions on page 32) and stir to combine.
2. In a food processor, process the melted chocolate mixture with the avocado, maple syrup, vanilla, and salt until very smooth. It should look like thick chocolate pudding at this point.
3. Transfer the frosting to a shallow bowl, cover, and refrigerate until thick and spreadable, about 3 hours. If needed, stir in a splash of nondairy milk if you'd like to thin the frosting for piping. The frosting can be stored in an airtight container in the fridge for 10 to 12 days.

TIP: To puree avocado, simply peel and pit a just-ripe avocado and then process briefly in your food processor before measuring.

Creamy Peanut Butter Frosting

. . . .

MAKES 3½ CUPS

If the world were ending, I might just whip up a batch of this frosting and eat it with a spoon. A thick and delicious peanut buttery frosting without the need for shortening and sugar? I'll take it. This recipe makes enough to pipe generous hills of frosting on a batch of cupcakes or to spread on a two-layer cake. Either way, it is divine. —N. A.

INGREDIENTS

1 (13.5-ounce) can full-fat coconut milk

1 cup pitted Medjool dates (see tip, page 199)

1 cup natural smooth peanut butter

1 teaspoon pure vanilla extract

½ teaspoon black-strap molasses

⅛ teaspoon sea salt

2 tablespoons melted coconut oil

INSTRUCTIONS

1. In a blender, combine the coconut milk and dates and blend on high speed until the dates are broken down.
2. Add the peanut butter, vanilla, molasses, salt, and coconut oil and blend until smooth. Transfer to a bowl, cover, and refrigerate until thick and spreadable, at least 4 hours. The frosting can be stored in an airtight container in the fridge for 10 to 12 days. After frosting your cake or cupcakes, keep them covered and refrigerated until ready to serve.

Thin Mint Sticks

· ·

MAKES 50 STICKS

These little sweets are not only a dream after-dinner treat but a truly spectacular garnish— slip a few sticks into an ice cream sundae, on top of a cheesecake, or into a minty milkshake. The flavor resembles everyone's favorite Girl Scout cookie, hence the name.

INGREDIENTS

½ cup raw cashews, soaked in water for 6 hours

1 cup coconut oil

¼ cup pure maple syrup

2 tablespoons unsweet-ened vanilla almond milk

1 tablespoon pure peppermint extract

7 ounces dairy-free dark chocolate, finely chopped

3 tablespoons coconut butter

INSTRUCTIONS

1. Drain and rinse the soaked cashews.
2. In a blender, combine the cashews, coconut oil, maple syrup, almond milk, and peppermint ex-tract and blend until very smooth.
3. Line an 8 x 8-inch square pan with parchment paper. Pour the mixture into the pan and spread it evenly with the back of a spoon or an offset spatula, or if it is thin enough to spread itself, just tap the bottom of the pan firmly on the counter to get rid of any air bubbles. Refrigerate until the mixture is firm enough to remove from the pan in one piece (at least 2 hours).
4. Remove the mixture from the pan. Using a sharp knife, score the square into three equal sections width-wise and then score each section crosswise into slices, about ¼ inch thick. Each stick should be about 2½ inches long and ¼ inch thick.
5. Firm the sticks in the freezer for at least 1 hour. In the meantime, prepare the chocolate coating by melting the chocolate and coconut butter in a double boiler (see instructions on page 32); stir until combined. Pour the chocolate mixture into a small, tall container to make it easier for dipping (like a mug or a heat-proof glass).
6. Remove half the sticks from the freezer. Place a piece of parchment paper on a cutting board, a baking sheet, or your counter.

7. Separate each stick by reslicing along the scored lines. Dip the stick into the chocolate, covering half of the stick with the coating, then place on the parchment paper. Once you have finished half the batch, return the sticks to the freezer to firm the chocolate. If you'd like to fully coat each stick, repeat the dipping process but dip the uncoated portion of the sticks into the chocolate. If not, repeat the dipping process with the remaining half of the sticks.

8. Store the firmed sticks in an airtight container in the freezer for up to 6 months. Serve them directly from the freezer, as they soften quickly at room temperature.

Peanut Butter Cups

. . . .

MAKES 14 PEANUT BUTTER CUPS

For those of you who miss Reese's peanut butter cups, here is a veganized version of everyone's favorite corner store treat. We pushed the filling to maximum peanut capacity and added dates and salt for an extra element of sweet and salty. We prefer using 70% cocoa dark chocolate for the coating but you can also use semisweet, if that's what you've got.

INGREDIENTS

½ cup dry-roasted unseasoned peanuts (see sidebar, page xx)

¼ cup pitted Medjool dates

¼ teaspoon sea salt

½ teaspoon pure vanilla extract

7 ounces dairy-free dark chocolate, finely chopped

3 tablespoons coconut butter, homemade (page 112) or store-bought

INSTRUCTIONS

1. In a food processor, process the peanuts until they turn into a smooth butter (about 5 minutes), stopping to scrape down the sides of the processor bowl as needed.

2. Add the dates, salt, and vanilla and continue to process until the dates are fully incorporated into the peanut butter. The mixture should be soft and stick together when pressed between your thumb and forefinger. Set the filling aside.

3. Melt the chocolate and coconut butter in a double boiler (see instructions on page 32) and stir to combine.

4. Line 14 wells of a mini cupcake tin with unbleached paper cupcake liners. Spoon 1 teaspoon of the melted chocolate into each liner. Tilt and twist each liner so the chocolate coats the sides of the liner, to about halfway up, and place them back in the pan.

5. Scoop out level teaspoons of the peanut filling and shape them into small discs. Place one peanut disc in the center of each chocolate-coated liner. Use the mini paper cups as a height guide, and try to make sure the top of the peanut disc is no taller than the chocolate coating. This prevents the filling from sticking out once it's topped with chocolate.

6. Spoon another teaspoon of melted chocolate on top of each peanut butter ball to cover completely. You may need to add a few drops more to get the chocolate level above the filling. Gently tap the pan on the counter to level the chocolate and release any air bubbles. Place the pan in the fridge to set, about 1 hour. Store the cups in an airtight container in the fridge for up to 1 month or freeze for up to 2 months.

Peanut Butter Cup Popcorn

. . . .

MAKES 8 CUPS

Since when do they sell big tubs of popcorn in bookstores? Turns out that was not the real question I needed to answer. Instead, it was how I could create a decadent vegan version of the peanut butter cup popcorn I had spotted among the stacks. That label had me dreaming about fluffy popcorn, in a sweet peanut butter coating, drizzled with a ribbon of dark chocolate. And now I've made those dreams come true. —L. P.

INGREDIENTS

2 teaspoons plus 2 tablespoons coconut oil

½ cup popcorn kernels

¼ cup smooth natural peanut butter

2 tablespoons pure maple syrup

½ teaspoon sea salt

1 teaspoon pure vanilla extract

4 ounces dairy-free chocolate, or ½ cup chocolate chips

INSTRUCTIONS

1. Preheat the oven to 300°F. Line two baking sheets with parchment paper.
2. In a large pot over medium-high heat, combine 2 teaspoons of the coconut oil and the popcorn kernels. Cover the pot and shake it back and forth across the burner to keep the kernels moving. Listen for the popping sound to slow down (3 to 5 minutes) then quickly pour the popcorn into a large bowl.
3. In a small saucepan, melt the remaining 2 tablespoons coconut oil, the peanut butter, maple syrup, and salt over medium-low heat; stir to combine. Remove from the heat and add the vanilla extract. Drizzle the mixture evenly over the popcorn and stir to coat.
4. Spread the popcorn over the prepared baking sheets. Bake for 15 minutes.
5. Finely chop the chocolate and melt it using a double boiler (see instructions on page 32). Drizzle the chocolate over the cooling popcorn. Transfer to the fridge to finish cooling, at least 30 minutes. Once completely cool, store in an airtight container at room temperature for up to 7 days.

White Chocolate Chips

The luscious combination of cashews and cacao butter make these chips rich and dreamy; however, that creamy texture means high heat is a nightmare. Instead of baking them into your cookies and muffins, save these chips for garnishing your cookies post-oven, or add them to raw desserts, sprinkle them atop frosted cakes, or slip some into your Mountain Climber's Mix (page 94).

INGREDIENTS

½ cup raw cashews, soaked in water for 6 hours

½ cup cacao butter, melted

¼ cup vanilla sugar (page 193), or ¼ cup cane sugar, pulsed fine in a blender plus 1 teaspoon pure vanilla extract

INSTRUCTIONS

1. Drain and rinse the soaked cashews.
2. In a food processor, grind the cashews until the nuts are broken down and just starting to form a paste.
3. In a blender, combine the ground cashews with the cacao butter and vanilla sugar and blend until completely smooth.

PIPING INSTRUCTIONS FOR PATIENT PEOPLE:

4. Transfer the mixture to a zip-top bag or a piping bag fitted with a small tip (e.g., #27) and refrigerate for 8 minutes to firm up. Depending on the temperature of your fridge, it might take a little longer to the get the chocolate firm enough to pipe. After 8 minutes, check it every 2 to 3 minutes until it is firm enough that you can pipe a perfect chip.
5. Warm up the piping bag for a few seconds by massaging it with your hands, until it feels pipable. If using a zip-top bag, cut off a small tip from one of the bottom corners, and twist the bag into the shape of a cone (like a piping bag).
6. Pipe small chocolate chips onto a piece of parchment paper (if you do this on top of a small cutting board, it is easier to move in and out of the freezer).

7. Once finished piping, transfer to the freezer for about 1 hour, until the chocolate chips easily release from the parchment paper and hold their form. Store in an airtight container in the fridge or freezer for up to 6 months.

CHOPPING INSTRUCTIONS FOR IMPATIENT PEOPLE:

4. Line an 8 x 8-inch pan with parchment paper. Pour the blended mixture to fill the pan evenly. Refrigerate until firm, about 1 hour.

5. Remove the firm white chocolate from the pan by pulling up on the parchment paper (releasing any sticking spots with a sharp knife). Place the chocolate on a large cutting board and chop into tiny squares (equivalent in size to chocolate chips). Separate the chips using your hands. Store in an airtight container in the fridge or freezer for up to 6 months.

Caramelized Chai Popcorn

MAKES 8 CUPS

One night in Portland, Oregon, at the good-bye gala for a big vegan conference, Nicole and I tasted a chai caramel corn that made both of us stop in our tracks. There, under the twinkling lights, surrounded by dancing and celebrating vegans, it was like our world had been paused as we savored every spicy bite. The next day, we tracked down more bags and squeezed as many as we could into our carry-ons. Back in Toronto, there was no way to avoid our mission: we needed to figure out how to replicate that special treat we had discovered so many miles away. Lucky for you, the tests are complete. We'd like to present this mind-blowing, sophisticated, spiced-up twist on the classic caramel corn. —L. P.

INGREDIENTS

2 teaspoons plus ⅓ cup coconut oil

½ cup popcorn kernels

1 cup coconut sugar

½ cup pure maple syrup

1 teaspoon ground cinnamon

½ teaspoon ground ginger

½ teaspoon freshly ground black pepper

½ teaspoon sea salt

¼ teaspoon ground cloves

Pinch of ground cardamon

2 teaspoons pure vanilla extract

INSTRUCTIONS

1. Preheat the oven to 300°F. Line two baking sheets with parchment paper.
2. In a large pot over medium-high heat, combine 2 teaspoons of the coconut oil and the popcorn kernels. Cover the pot and shake it back and forth across the burner to keep the kernels moving. Listen for the popping sound to slow down (3 to 5 minutes) then quickly remove from heat and pour the popcorn into a large bowl.
3. In a small pot, combine the coconut sugar, maple syrup, cinnamon, ginger, pepper, salt, cloves, and cardamom and stir over medium heat until the sugar has dissolved and a thin, pourable liquid has developed. Simmer for 5 minutes. Remove from the heat and add the vanilla.
4. Pour the sauce over the popcorn and toss to coat.
5. Spread the popcorn into a single layer on the prepared backing sheets. Bake for 15 minutes. About halfway through, toss the popcorn around the pan using a spoon. Remove from the oven and let it cool completely. Store in an airtight container at room temperature for up to 7 days.

Cookie Dough (for baking or eating)

. . . .

MAKES 30 COOKIES

There is no question: cookie dough is awesome. Although for decades, vegans have been licking the spoon coated in uncooked cookie dough without fear, just recently we've seen prepared vegan versions popping up in grocery store coolers. So this make-at-home version was specially designed to delight you by the spoonful or to satisfy with a toothsome texture when baked up fresh. Even though they're oil-free, you won't miss it. As our testers claimed, these just might the best cookies you've ever eaten.

INGREDIENTS

¾ cup smooth natural peanut or almond butter

2 tablespoons pear sauce or applesauce

1 teaspoon pure vanilla extract

½ cup rolled oats, pulsed into a flour using a food processor or blender

½ cup raw almonds, pulsed into a meal using a food processor or a blender

½ cup maple sugar

¼ cup coconut sugar

1 teaspoon baking powder

½ teaspoon sea salt

⅓ cup dairy-free chocolate chips

INSTRUCTIONS

1. In a small bowl, stir together the peanut butter, pear sauce, vanilla, and 6 tablespoons water.
2. In a medium bowl, stir together the oat flour, almond meal, maple sugar, coconut sugar, baking powder, salt, and chocolate chips. Add the wet mixture and stir to combine.
3. Refrigerate the dough for 1 hour or up to overnight in an airtight container. (If you just want to eat it with a spoon, you're done here.)
4. If you want cookies: Preheat the oven to 350°F. Line two baking sheets with parchment paper.
5. Scoop out 1 tablespoon of the dough and place it on a prepared baking sheet. Press down gently to slightly flatten the dough. Repeat until you have 30 small cookies, evenly spaced and divided among the two trays.
6. Bake for 13 to 14 minutes. Let cool on the baking sheets for 2 minutes before transferring to a cooling rack. Store the cookies in an airtight container at room temperature for up to 5 days, or in the freezer for 3 to 4 weeks.

TIP: These are small cookies that freeze beautifully. Make a big batch and always have cookies handy to garnish desserts, slip into a sundae, or snack on with a glass of warm almond milk. For ready-to-bake cookies any time, portion out tablespoon-size scoops onto a baking sheet and freeze. Once firm, the cookies can be stored in an airtight container in the freezer and baked a few at time whenever you're in the mood.

TRY THIS: All out of almonds? This recipe can also be made with 1 cup whole wheat pastry flour in place of the ½ cup almonds and ½ cup oats.

Cookie Dough (page 220) and
Easy Almond Milk (page 38)

Almond Pulp Cookie Crumbs

MAKES 1 CUP

A fantastic way to use up all that leftover almond pulp, these sweet, cinnamony, all-purpose cookie crumbs can be used in place of store-bought cookie crumbs for ice cream cakes, pie crusts, or as a topping for parfaits or fruit crisp. Feel free to double the recipe if you have enough pulp!

INGREDIENTS

¾ cup almond pulp, left over from making Basic Nut/Seed Milk (page 37)

¼ cup finely shredded coconut

1 teaspoon ground cinnamon

¼ teaspoon sea salt

3 tablespoons pure maple syrup

2 tablespoons melted coconut oil

½ teaspoon pure vanilla extract

INSTRUCTIONS

1. Preheat the oven to 300°F. Line a rimmed baking sheet with parchment paper.
2. In a bowl, combine the almond pulp, shredded coconut, cinnamon, and salt.
3. In another small bowl, whisk together the maple syrup, coconut oil, and vanilla. Pour the liquid ingredients into the bowl with the almond pulp mixture and stir to combine. Use the back of your spoon to press the liquid into the almond pulp and then break it up into crumbs.
4. Spread the crumbs evenly over the prepared baking sheet. Break apart any larger crumbs so they are all close to the same size. Bake for about 45 minutes, stirring two or three times throughout, until golden and dry but not yet crispy. Remove from the oven and let cool completely.
5. Pulse the crumbs briefly in a food processor or blender. The cookie crumbs can be stored in an airtight container at room temperature for about 2 months, or in the freezer for up to 4 months.

Cinnamon Graham Crackers

MAKES ABOUT 30 CRACKERS

I first learned the stunningly simple technique of toasting flour to bring out its flavor from Fran Costigan, vegan pastry chef extraordinaire and instructor at the Natural Gourmet Institute in NYC, where I studied. This technique is key to the flavor of these crackers and is our preference to using graham flour, the ingredient that is traditionally used but not easy to find. Packed with whole grains and a good dose of cinnamon, these crackers bake up crisp so they hold up to all sorts of decadent desserts, like the Lemon-Blueberry Icebox Cake on page 227. They're also great on their own, and are especially good paired with tea. —N. A.

INGREDIENTS

2 cups whole wheat pastry flour

⅓ cup coconut sugar

1 teaspoon ground cinnamon

½ teaspoon sea salt

¼ teaspoon baking soda

¼ cup melted coconut oil

¼ cup pure maple syrup

2 teaspoons pure vanilla extract

1 teaspoon black-strap molasses

INSTRUCTIONS

1. Preheat the oven to 350°F. Line a large rimmed baking sheet with parchment paper.
2. Spread out the whole wheat flour on the prepared baking sheet and toast for 10 minutes, stirring halfway through. Let cool completely (place the flour in a large bowl in the fridge or freezer to cool it quickly).
3. In a large bowl, whisk together the toasted flour, coconut sugar, cinnamon, salt, and baking soda.
4. In another small bowl, whisk together ¼ cup warm water, the coconut oil, maple syrup, vanilla, and molasses. Pour into the bowl with the dry ingredients and stir until a soft, pliable dough forms.
5. Place the dough on a large piece of parchment paper (you can use the same one you used to toast the flour) and use your hands to shape it into a rough rectangle. Place another piece of parchment paper on top and use a rolling pin to roll from the center out. As you roll out the dough, rotate the paper so you roll to produce a relatively even 12 x 16-inch rectangle, about ¼ to ⅛ inch thick. Remove the top piece of parchment paper and trim the edges of the dough using a sharp knife or pastry cutter.

6. Cut the dough into 2-inch squares by making vertical and thin horizontal cuts across it. Using the prongs of a fork, prick each cracker a couple of times. Reroll and cut the leftover scraps of dough, if desired.

7. Transfer the crackers, still on the parchment paper, to the baking sheet. Bake for 15 to 18 minutes. Let cool completely. They are a little soft right out of the oven but will crisp up as they cool. The graham crackers can be stored in an airtight container at room temperature for about 2 weeks or in the freezer for up to 2 months.

Lemon-Blueberry Icebox Cake

MAKES ONE 8 X 8-INCH CAKE

At the tail-end of a historically frigid winter, we created this recipe to transport us to a big, beautiful porch at sunset on a sweltering summer night, where we would serve this by the spoonful to all of our favorite people and top each bowl with berries as the sunset painted the sky pink. Since you don't need to turn on your oven to make this cake, it seems ideal for those nights when all you want to eat is something cool, covered in berries. And because no matter how hard you try, you can't make this look like a perfectly composed confection, you can just relax, spoon out a big luscious lump, and invite over all your friends to share.

And if you live somewhere where winter lasts so long that you can no longer believe summer exists, make a batch, put on a sweater, and escape.

INGREDIENTS

1 recipe Cinnamon Graham Crackers (page 225)

1 recipe Lemon Curd (page 196)

1 cup blueberries (frozen work best—defrost in a strainer to remove any excess liquid before using)

1 recipe Whipped Cream (page 40)

Fresh blueberries, for garnish

INSTRUCTIONS

1. In an 8 x 8-inch square baking pan, make a single layer of graham crackers. If there are spaces left between the crackers, break off pieces of the remaining crackers to fill them in.
2. Spoon half of the lemon curd on top of the graham cracker layer and spread evenly with the back of a spoon or an offset spatula.
3. Sprinkle half of the blueberries evenly across the top of the lemon curd layer.
4. Spoon half of the whipped cream on top of the blueberry layer. Spread gently using the back of a spoon or an offset spatula.
5. Repeat steps 1 through 4.
6. Cover with a piece of plastic wrap and refrigerate for at least 8 hours. This allows the graham crackers to soften and become cakelike. This is a scoopable dessert. Serve in bowls with a few fresh blueberries on top.

Ice Cream Sandwiches

MAKES 6 SANDWICHES

The best ice cream sandwiches use cookies that stay soft and chewy even when frozen. In this case, we took that basic requirement and ramped things up a couple of notches by creating a vegan, gluten-free cookie that tastes like a decadent brownie and sandwiching two around a creamy, coconutty, vanilla ice cream. You're welcome.

INGREDIENTS

½ cup almonds, ground into a meal using a food processor or blender

½ cup rolled oats, ground into a flour using a food processor or blender

½ cup cocoa powder

½ cup maple sugar or cane sugar

¼ cup coconut sugar

1 teaspoon baking powder

½ teaspoon sea salt

¾ cup coconut butter, homemade (page 112) or store-bought, softened

2 tablespoons unsweetened applesauce

1 recipe Vanilla Bean Ice Cream (page 62), softened for 30 minutes at room temperature.

INSTRUCTIONS

1. Preheat the oven to 350°F. Line a baking sheet with parchment paper.
2. In a medium bowl, combine the almond meal, oat flour, cocoa powder, maple sugar, coconut sugar, baking powder, and salt.
3. In a small bowl, whisk together the coconut butter, applesauce, and ¼ cup water.
4. Pour the wet mixture into the bowl with the dry mixture and stir to combine.
5. Pour the dough onto the baking sheet and spread it into a rectangle, about ½ inch thick, with an offset spatula. Bake for 10 to 12 minutes.
6. Cut into 12 individual rectangle cookies. Let cool.
7. Spoon about 3 tablespoons of ice cream onto half of the cookies. Add a cookie on top to make 6 sandwiches. Wrap each sandwich in plastic wrap or waxed paper and store in the freezer in an airtight container for up to 2 months.

TRY THIS: Prefer a triple chocolate explosion dessert experience? Swap out the Vanilla Bean Ice Cream for Chocolate (page 63), and before firming, press the sides of the ice cream sandwiches into a tray of chocolate chips. Happy times are here again.

TIP: If you have a pizza cutter, it does an amazing job slicing through the warm cookies. If not, you can use a sharp knife or have fun with different cookie cutters.

Ice Cream Cone Confections

. . . .

MAKES 6 CONES

There was a time when you could get a vegan treat just like this at your health food store. But for some reason, its availability was so fleeting that we never even got to try a bite. So, we've given up on waiting on the whims of others—we've put our DIY spirit to good use and created a recipe you can count on. Vegan cones for everyone!

INGREDIENTS

1 cup dairy-free chocolate chips

2 tablespoons coconut oil

6 sugar cones (read the ingredients to be sure they are vegan)

1 recipe Vanilla Bean Ice Cream (page 62), softened at room temperature for 30 minutes

¼ cup toasted pecans, hazelnuts, or salted peanuts, finely chopped

INSTRUCTIONS

1. Melt the chocolate chips and coconut oil using a double boiler (see instructions on page 32) and stir to combine. Set the bowl on the counter for 10 minutes to cool.
2. Spoon a generous tablespoon of chocolate into each cone. Roll it around in your hands to coat the inside of the cone with a thin layer of chocolate. Turn the cone upside down over the bowl of melted chocolate to let any of the excess chocolate drain out. Let stand for 10 minutes to firm (if your home is hot and humid, let firm in the fridge).
3. Scoop the ice cream into each cone, pressing firmly to pack it all in, with about 1 to 2 inches above the top of the cone. Smooth the sides and top with an offset spatula, just like icing a cake. Freeze upright for an hour (the wire shelf in many freezers works like a charm).
4. Spoon 2 teaspoons of the chocolate onto each ice cream–filled cone and smooth with the back of the spoon or an offset spatula.
5. Sprinkle the top of each cone with chopped nuts, pressing lightly to ensure they stick to the chocolate. Return to the freezer for 30 to 60 minutes to firm up the chocolate. Serve or wrap each cone in waxed paper or plastic wrap and store in an airtight container in the freezer for up to 2 months.

Ice Cream Cone Confections (page xx)

Acknowledgments

What started out as a casual introduction at the launch party of Jae Steele's *Ripe from Around Here* at a community center hidden in the west end of Toronto blossomed into a friendship that neither of us had ever expected. We soon became blogger buddies partnering to create online recipe challenges, local outreach events, food demos, e-cookbooks, and magazine articles, and encouraging each other in our individual pursuits through raw chef school, culinary teachings in foreign countries, vegan baking programs, nutrition courses, and food photography ventures. Our shared passion for vegan food, healthy living, and creating community has been a critical source of support over the past six years. This partnership has made possible a lot of exciting projects and fun adventures, but we never would have imagined back in 2010 that it would also enable us both to realize the dream of sharing our recipes with the world through publishing a cookbook. It has been a journey, and we're so glad we had each other at every step.

Much like it takes a village to raise a child, the birth of this cookbook took the support and hard work of an entire cast of allies and experts. We would not have been able to do this without an awesome agent, an amazing publisher, a brilliant editor, an enthusiastic publicist, a gifted marketing manager, talented designers, a team of committed recipe testers, generous and loving friends and family, and the most incredible partners in the world.

We would like to thank the team at St. Martin's Press for making this book happen, including Michael Flamini, Vicki Lame, Marie Estrada, Michelle Cashman, Crystal Ben, and Steven Seighman. You are all remarkable individuals and we are humbled by your gentle, practical, and always collaborative approach to guiding this project. You made this experience seem easy, supportive, and fun for us first-time authors. A very special thanks to our agent, Steve

Troha, for believing in this book from the start, helping us to hone our skills and ideas, and continuing to be there for every little question and request.

There are no words to describe how much gratitude we have in our hearts for Blake Bezan and Sascha von Nickisch-Rosenegk. Blake, thank you for your patience with Nicole when she got frustrated with herself or a recipe that just wouldn't work, for your encouragement when she got discouraged, and for making her laugh when Eli jumped up on the counter and onto her perfectly rolled cookie dough. Thank you for cleaning the house, going to the store when she ran out of almonds, taste testing whatever she put in front of you, and, most important, for being her biggest fan. Sascha, thank you for making big, huge, amazing kale salads when Lisa was too tired from recipe testing to even think about cooking. Thank you for your honest feedback, your participation in hours of brainstorming and problem solving, your enthusiastic belief in *DIY Vegan*, and for being an endless source of love and support to Lisa. She is still praising the red-light gods that brought you into her life.

Thank you to our families, who happily ate the leftover cashew cheese, ice cream, crackers, and chocolate cake (oh, so much chocolate cake!) and who understood when looming deadlines meant we were hunkered down in our kitchens rather than visiting you. Special thanks to Nicole's in-laws, Bob and Mary Lynn, and Scott and Kathryn. Your love and ongoing support mean the world to Nicole. To Nicole's stepmom, Lisa, thank you for teaching her that food is about celebration, community, and love. Wray and Catherine, thank you for being you. Your combination of influences has made Nicole who she is today. Thank you to Lisa's mom, Teresa Pitman, who shared her insights on the whole publishing process and read every word of the manuscript. Your encouragement, expertise, advice, and love have been instrumental in the success of this book and our confidence to make it happen. Thank you to Lisa's siblings, their partners, and their children (Matt, Es, Dan, Ali, Jeremy, Heather, Sebastian, Callista, Xavier, Keagan, Mackenzie, and Dexter) for always being excited to try Lisa's new culinary creations and for cheering us on throughout this whole endeavor.

A clinking of wineglasses to Nicole's ever fabulous BS Club family, Emily Taylor, Roy Hennig, Jason Kogan, Miranda Steele, Gord Lucas, David Alencuin, Robin Ward, Amelia Facchin, David Ward, Steve Wolpert, Eva Chau, and Mike Drach, and to her BFF, Natalya Anderson, who all bring so much joy and laughter to her life. Thank you for being there for Nicole when she needed taste testers, an ear, a fun night out, or a large glass of chardonnay at the end of a long day.

Gracious gratitude to Lisa's loves, the Po5 women, who have proven a steadfast source of honesty, encouragement, and wine over the decades. A special shout-out to Hannah and Christine, who both listened to the trials and tribulations of recipe testing for far too many hours. Your patience, love, and hilarious sense of humor have been Lisa's saving grace. And appreciation to all of Lisa's colleagues (most notably Janos, Arlene, Mandy, Sean, Jamie, Wayne, Rory, and Bill), who tested treats, signed up for lunch clubs, requested recipes, and asked almost every day for the past decade when she would get around to writing a cookbook. Without your belief in this project, it would never have become a reality.

The feedback from our recipe-testing team was invaluable in the development of these recipes. Huge thanks to Dianne Wenz, Sarah Wise, Lydia Grossov, Monika Soria Caruso, Gina Van Hyfte, Carrie Horsburgh, Michelle Bishop, Cintia Bock, Eve Lynch, Dan Pitman, Marika Collins, and Cindy Reichle (who also lent us her amazing design skills). You guys are incredible. This book would not be the reliable resource it is today without your tireless efforts and opinions.

A nod to the talented vegan superwomen who guided us with their infinite wisdom, advice, referrals, and recommendations: Dreena Burton, Fran Costigan, Ricki Heller, Allyson Kramer, Terry Romero, Isa Moskowitz, Angela Liddon, Gena Hamshaw, J. L. Fields, and Victoria Moran. And to the incredible vegan community worldwide, both virtual and in person, your enthusiasm, steady engagement, and shared passions are infectious and fill our hearts and lives with a much-needed sense of community. Together, we are an unstoppable force—Ambassadors of Compassion! Thank you for supporting our efforts to change the world for humans, the animals, and the environment.

Closer to home, a big thank-you to the Toronto Vegetarian Association for their continued support of our dreams and efforts.

Index